AN EVERYDAY HERO

HOW TO FIND AND DEVELOP THE HERO WITHIN

Douglas Pyszka

SPECIAL THANKS

Special thanks to my Lord and Savior Jesus, whom I love with all my heart, My Father God, who is so good to me and the Holy Spirit who has empowered me to complete this task.

I want to thank Lisa Schmidt for her diligence in editing this book and helping me to dot my "I's" and cross my "T's" and for helping me to connect with people in the best way possible.

A special thanks to my wonderful loving wife Fiona. Her support and cooperation towards me emboldens me to step out and do great and mighty things. She has helped bring this project to reality. I am grateful to be married to such a mighty woman of God. I also want to thank my two sons, Gabriel and Josiah who have allowed me to dedicate extra time to complete this project.

CONTENTS

INTRODUCTION

This book was written on the belief that it is possible for every man to be a hero with God. Many people are fascinated with heroes. We appreciate their super qualities, skills, and abilities to fight evil, help people, fulfill their mission and save the world.

Heroes are exemplary figures who inspire the common man. Secretly, we wish we were like them being able to do what they do with such grace and finesse. The truth is you can be a hero for God! God calls people, just like you, and empowers them with supernatural ability by His Holy Spirit to be everyday heroes for Him. An everyday hero is a person who uses what God has given him, does what God commands and becomes what God wants him to be every day.

Here are some questions to ponder about heroes: Is a hero someone we simply admire, respect or look up to or is he more than that? Is a hero some kind of superhero with super powers? Is it necessary to have a lot of money and fame to be a hero? Does fame alone make someone a good role model? What is involved in being a hero? Can you call yourself a hero? Why does the word hero make some people feel awkward or uncomfortable? Have you had a hero in your life? What kind of difference can a hero make?

If you believe in God, within you are qualities that make you extraordinary. If you don't believe in God, then maybe it is time to change your belief. It is my desire to help you recognize those divine qualities, see them activated in your life and help you become an everyday hero for God. In the following pages, you will learn what a hero is and how he can fight *and win by faith*. We will examine descriptions of Biblical characters that faced tough challenges and *overcame* them by being an everyday hero for God. I believe that God wants **you to be a hero for Him**.

DOUGLAS PYSZKA

Chapter 1

QUALITIES OF EVERYDAY HEROES

One quality that every man must have to be an everyday hero is faith in God and Jesus Christ. The greatest hero of all time is Jesus Christ. He is loved & admired by many. He was willing to sacrifice His life to save others. He is extraordinary because He saved the world from eternal destruction. Jesus skillfully and successfully accomplished His mission and defeated sin, the devil, death and the grave. Faith in Jesus Christ enables you to become the hero God has designed you to be. Faith activates your super hero qualities and empowers to you to carry out God's will.

God is looking for someone just like you, who will use his God-given abilities and characteristics to: face challenges, overcome, win, to influence others, to be involved in godly pursuits and to help others fulfill their divine purpose. God's Word and Spirit make you extraordinary and they actively work in those who believe in Jesus Christ in order to become be a godly hero.

Heroes come in all shapes and sizes so would you be able to recognize a hero if you saw one? What does a hero look like? Can you discern the heroic qualities that are within you? Everyone has at least one heroic quality or more within them. This book will help you find and develop the hero within you. As we discuss different characters of the Bible, you will see qualities and characteristics' that will stand out to help you understand what a hero has and who a hero is which will make it easier to recognize them.

A hero is a person who possesses certain qualities and abilities that cause him to stand out from the crowd. He is noted for feats of courage; nobility of purpose; an understanding of his mission; a willingness to risk his life to save others and face tough challenges willingly. A hero faces challenges with God-like qualities like strength, character and ability to do things that are supernatural. He endures hardships, stands up for what is right, protects the innocent, helps others and fights for a good cause.

The Bible describes the actions of a hero very well. A hero is watchful and alert; he has a firm faith in God; he is brave and strong (1 Corinthians 16:13-14). A hero casts his cares to God and trusts Him completely; he is sober and clear-minded; he is vigilant, persevering and resists evil with faith; he needs God's grace; he continually develops his ability to fight evil and increases in knowledge; he is accepts and recognizes who God made him to be (1 Peter 5:6-11). A hero confronts and fights evil; he has special equipment to defend and protect himself; he overcomes temptation; he stands strong even if he is alone; he embraces truth and righteousness; he has a mind and will to win; he can stop his enemies when they attack and triumphs in all things (Ephesians 6:12-18)

Every hero must be brave, ready to stand and prepared to fight. A hero is not intimidated by any enemy and must be determined to win. Determination makes the difference between the impossible and possible.

A hero is committed to his God–given mission, which is his purpose. Find your purpose in God and stick with it. A hero also needs to endure and not quit when the going gets tough, but keep going. A true hero will simply outlast all opposition. Uncommon valor enables a hero to face challenges without fear. As a hero, you will act selflessly and sacrificially to save others. Finally, every hero should be humble and trust in God alone. Humility protects a hero from pride.

A hero stands out because he is willing to use the power he has when it is needed most to help others. God has given every man super hero abilities that are waiting to be called upon to face challenges and win. Get ready because your opportunity to stand out may be around the corner.

A hero is action-oriented, ready to jump in to face danger and help people. A hero puts his faith into action every day by applying his knowledge of God to every circumstance of life. He goes into action with no expectation of material gain or recognition even risking his physical comfort, social stature or quality of life. When others stand still, a hero stands out by speaking up, acting to help and staying the course.

You may not think of yourself as a hero because of your faults, failures and facades. Others may even agree with that assessment of you, but you can become a hero every day by believing in the Lord Jesus Christ. When Christ comes into your heart, He releases the hero within and brings him forth in power. Get rid of the thoughts that tell you what you're not and embrace the truth in Jesus, and become what He has made you to be!

Chapter 2

AN EVERYDAY HERO IS A MAN OF FAITH

All the men you will study in this book are men who had faith in God. Without faith, a hero will fail because he will not please God. It is important to understand some things about faith in order to become an everyday hero for God.

Faith in God transforms you into a mighty super hero and brings the power of God to you. Jesus Christ is the author and finisher of our faith and He is the greatest hero of all time. He is loved, admired and looked up to by many who believe in Him. Jesus fully completed His mission and sacrificed Himself to save the whole world. The work He did was miraculous and supernatural, and made Him stand out from the crowd. He saved the world from eternal destruction. His character was impeccable and He used His power to defeat all His enemies, even conquering death, hell and the grave. Put your faith in Jesus and trust in His Word wholeheartedly. The Word of God and the Spirit of God enable you to be the hero God designed you to be. Faith in God activates your super hero qualities that are in you.

Understanding what faith is will help you become the hero that God wants you to be. Faith is: hearing God's Word; receiving it into your soul; believing it with your whole heart and acting on what it says. The Bible has a whole chapter, Hebrews eleven, about people who were faith heroes. It gives us a picture of people who had faith in God and did amazing heroic things in this earth.

The Bible tells us in Hebrews Ch. 11 that faith is the substance of things hoped and the evidence of things unseen. Faith is being sure of what you hoped for and certain of what you do not see. Faith in God is an important super hero quality that you need in order to be an everyday hero.

Here are some other translations of Hebrews 11:1 that will help you understand faith better.

- Faith is the assurance of things hoped for, the conviction of things not seen (NASB).
- Faith is the confident assurance that what we hope for is going to happen. It is the evidence of things we cannot see (NLT).
- The Amplified Bible describes faith as being the assurance, the confirmation and the title deed for what we hope for. It is the proof of things we do not see and the conviction of their reality. Faith perceives as real fact what has not been revealed to the senses.
- Faith is of things hoped for a confidence, of matters not seen a conviction (YLT)

Faith in God strengthens your confidence, which is necessary to be a super hero. As you hear God's Word, faith comes to your heart and requires you to take action. If you don't act on God's Word, then your faith is dead and powerless.

According to Hebrews 11:6, Faith pleases God. Through faith, the invisible becomes visible. What you see by faith becomes a reality in your life. Faith is durable and everlasting and you can live by it. Develop your *lifestyle of faith* and be skilled in looking to God, trusting in Him and performing His Word every day and you can be a super hero for God.

You may doubt whether or not you could be an everyday hero for God. Put your doubt out and realize, by faith, that you can be anything God wants you to be. Choose to live by your faith in God today. Faith heroes are in demand because people need help, the world needs to be saved and God needs you to rise up, stand for truth, justice and righteousness. This book can help you discover your unique abilities, your God-given talents and develop your skill in being God's hero. It is not time to shrink back but to step up, live by faith and shine for the Lord! (Hebrews 10:37-39)

How an Everyday Hero Fights by Faith

An everyday hero fights battles in life with the weapons of faith. He does not fight people but the spirits that influence the people's behavior. The Bible is your guide and gives you a divine strategy about how to fight the fight of faith in Ephesians chapter six. God will reward your faith. Being a hero means, you know your mission in life as God has revealed it to you, and you passionately live to achieve it by faith.

The enemies in the fight of faith are not people but principalities, powers, evil spirits ruling in dark places and wicked spirits in the atmosphere. You are strengthened by God's Word and Spirit to stand against evil and defeat these enemies. God provided you with supernatural armor to fight in faith, stand against evil and win.

Another weapon you have is prayer that unleashes an aerial assault on the devil, demons and all evil spirits. You have many types of prayer at your disposal. As a skilled warrior, you can be highly trained in all your spiritual weapons you possess. Develop your skill now (Ephesians 6:10-18)

As a hero, you are *confident in your heart and mind that you are a winner,* and you discipline your body to uphold God's standards. Practice the truth every day and be a good example for others to follow so you do not become disqualified from receiving God's reward (1 Corinthians 9:25-27)

As the **fight of faith unfolds**, do not place heavy burdens on others or act offensively in anything. Protect your integrity and remain blameless by doing what is right in God's sight. As an everyday hero, serve God faithfully, be available to carry out His divine call and receive divine power which gives you supernatural ability.

Winning by faith requires you to be strong in God's Word and His Spirit. The strength you receive from God helps you endure hard things. God helps you to trust Him wholeheartedly even in dark times. Godly character keeps you strong in faith and should consist of: love, joy, peace, longsuffering, kindness, goodness, faithfulness, gentleness and self-control. God arms you with supernaturally strong weapons and when you speak God's Words, God's authoritative and creative power is released in the earth (2

Corinthians 6:3-12)

The fight of faith is not fought with human or fleshly weapons, but with the weapons that come from God. They are powerful enough to overthrow and demolish strongholds that get built up in the mind. Fight in faith by contesting worldly arguments, theories and thinking. Reject proud and lofty ideas that go against God's Word. Capture and arrest evil thoughts, ideas and suggestions and command them to be silent. The thoughts you think, the words you speak and the actions you take need to reflect Christ and His standards. Do what is right in God's sight. Stop wicked and evil thoughts that come to you by refusing to act on them and they will be aborted (2 Corinthians 10:3-7).

It is important for an everyday hero to think correctly. As a hero, you must be sober-minded to fight by faith. Encourage, urge and build others up and consider them before yourself. When a challenge arises that looks overwhelming, build a team of people you know and work together to overcome the challenge, and win.

As a hero, you should lead by example. Treat people in authority respectfully and appreciate leaders who are doing God's will. Resist the temptation to take revenge on those who do wrong and do not repay evil with evil. The Lord will avenge you so, leave that up to Him. Be like Stephen, a disciple in the early church, in Acts chapter seven, who forgave those who stoned him to death just like Jesus did on the cross. Stephen saw Jesus standing at God's right hand, who gave him a standing ovation for how he stood for faith and forgave his accusers. Be kind to people and seek their good. Energize your faith with joy and be persistent in prayer (1 Thessalonians 5:8-17)

Being an everyday hero for God means you are a person with impeccable and trustworthy character. Allow God to train you and develop your skill in being a holy soldier. Learn how to use God's Word and Spirit to fight a good fight of faith. A good fight is one you win. You must hold fast to faith and lean on God confidently. Maintain a clean conscience and a clean heart by staying close to Jesus (1 Timothy 1:18-20)

As you apply these truths to your life and your life to these truths, you will be an everyday hero for God being able to accomplish great things in this earth. God transforms you into a mighty warrior through His Word and Spirit, like Clark Kent is transformed into Superman.

God is looking for you to use the super hero qualities He has given you to step up, help others, face challenges in life and overcome. With faith in God, you can be delivered from danger, influence others to pursue God's plan for their life and help them reach their destiny. Faith in God makes you extraordinary so you can be an everyday hero for God.

Chapter 3

THE HERO CONNECTION: TV HERO VS. BIBLE HERO

The traits that are modeled by comic book heroes like: courage, truth, integrity and justice reflect the real traits that are possessed by Christian heroes. You may be familiar with the following comic book heroes: the X-men, Spider Man, Batman, Superman, Daredevil, Fantastic Four, Iron Man, Green Lantern, Thor and Captain America. They are heroes who possessed super powers and special skills, and they fought against evil. All of these have been very popular movies.

Movies that are about heroes are very popular in our culture because people are fascinated by heroes, they view them as role-models and desire to be like them in how they use their super powers to fight evil. The problem with this is, that the characters in movies like these are not real and you need to pattern your life after real people.

God creates real heroes. His ultimate hero is Jesus who did more for humanity than anyone ever will. Jesus is a real person and is the most powerful super hero ever. Jesus shares his super powers with anyone who believes in Him wholeheartedly. By faith, you can be a hero just like Him.

Captain America, The First Avenger, was a very popular movie that came out in the last few years. The movie is about finding a perfect soldier that could turn the tide of war and cause good to win over evil. In the movie, a new breed of super-soldier was created through the development of a special serum. The military leaders and scientists took a skinny, scrawny young man, Steve Rogers, who was courageous, brave and kind, and turned him into a super hero with super strength, ability and agility. Prior to becoming a super hero he was encouraged to remain to be the man he always was, a man of good moral character, honest and one who refused to quit.

When your abilities cause you to stand out from the crowd, you could be tempted to be prideful. Captain America could have become prideful with his newly acquired skills. Instead of being prideful, he remained humble and did what is right and honest in helping people.

You must resist the temptation to lift yourself up or credit yourself for the great things you do or how God uses you to help others. Pride will knock you down to the ground and destroy you because God resists the proud, but He gives grace to the humble.

Acquiring supernatural ability should not take away from the quality of your character. God values godly character above the great things you can do or accomplish. A godly hero possesses character traits that reflect God throughout his life. Although Steve Rogers became the super soldier Captain America, he also stayed true to who he was and he did what he believed to be right. With great power comes great responsibility. Use your God-given power to help others instead of using them to promote yourself.

God will help you to overcome your weaknesses, short comings and faults so you can display His supernatural powers to face challenges, overcome them and win over adversity. God will give you an encounter with Him that will transform your life in amazing ways, enabling you to be *an everyday hero for God*.

One person really can make a positive difference in this world to make it better. Those who know God will be strong and do great exploits (Daniel 11:32). Daniel influenced a nation to believe in God instead of idols. Joseph saved a nation from starvation and extinction because God gave him insight into the future. Abraham father a new nation and a new race of people. People who *know the Lord God* are transformed from **ordinary into extraordinary**. All things are possible to him who believes (Mark 9:23).

Now, truth be told, we all want to be heroes. We all want to make that difference, in that moment of time, that will dramatically impact a situation where: people need help; you can foster change; keep someone safe and stand up for what is right and just. We all simply desire the ability and the power to act freely and without restraint to make this kind of difference. You can do this with *God in you.*

God is calling you to step up and be an everyday hero for Him. **You can do it** and **He will help you**. God wants to make a difference in this world through you. Through Him, you can be a super hero who makes a positive difference.

THE EVERYDAY HERO CHALLENGE

The heart of the *"Everyday Hero Challenge"* is to become a true hero by inviting Jesus Christ into your heart, accept Him as Lord of your life and be a committed Christian. If you are a Christian, then *believe you can be an everyday hero* by: faithfully serving God every day; using your God-given abilities to face challenges and win; confronting evil; doing what is right in God's sight; helping others and making a difference in your world by allowing God to help, guide and strengthen you.

As a hero, be committed to do what is right and just according to God. Trust God wholeheartedly to provide you with what you need every day. As an everyday hero, you will not walk alone, but God will walk with you. He is very interested in your success and will help you to do great exploits.

As you study the heroes in this book, you will learn how they: had significance; were assigned a mission; faced challenges and used their God-given abilities to make a big difference in the lives of others and also in themselves. God has given abilities to you to help others; enhance your own life and to make a difference in the world. Choose to be a hero for God in your heart by continuing to stand strong every day.

My challenge to all who read this book: Be a *hero*, not a *bystander!* Be an "*everyday*" person who is willing to keep your eyes, ears and heart open "*every day*" to any opportunity that may demand heroism; call you to arise and meet a challenge or help others in some way.

I thank you for being a person willing to make this kind of commitment and hold yourself accountable in fulfilling it — for others, for organizations, for issues you care about in God's Kingdom. Your commitment to this challenge will allow you to live an extraordinary life making the difference that needs to be made. Stay engaged and "**Be an Every Day Hero for God!**"

THE HERO'S PLEDGE

I recommend you make this a regular confession for your life.

I commit to be an everyday hero for God by knowing God, His will, His way and following after Him with all my heart. I will use my God-given abilities as God leads me to help people and serve in His Kingdom. I am strong in character that promotes righteousness and justice believing and upholding what God says. I am an everyday hero for God. I live by faith and can do all things through Christ who strengthens me.

DOUGLAS PYSZKA

Chapter 4

AN EVERDAY HERO IS INVINCIBLE

An invincible hero is one who is: victorious over challenges, unconquerable, triumphant over difficulties; maintaining a strong position throughout your life. You are only invincible, if Jesus is the Lord of your life.

God is your source of strength and power. Through Him, you can do amazing things. If Jesus is your Lord, you are God's hero and He makes you invincible just like He made the heroes before you invincible. You must believe what the Bible says is absolutely true and applicable for you, and visualize yourself as a godly super hero.

The Bible is full of true stories that describe what it means to be an invincible hero. The Bible is a book of champions, overcomers and winners.

Through God _you will do valiantly_ and your _enemies will be your bread_ (Psalm 60:12; Numbers 14:9). God will transform you into Prince Valiant and will cause you to be courageous, bold and fearless. You will beat all the enemies you face for they will be like bread to you which is soft and easily consumed.

You may have been afflicted many times but **your enemy will not prevail against you. You can chase your enemies and they shall fall before you** (Psalm 129:2). As an everyday hero, you will continue to rise up no matter how much trouble you face, how much you have suffered or how distressed you are. **In your weakest moment, your enemy will not win against you**. Rise up and chase your enemies for they shall be defeated.

**Five can chase a hundred and a hundred shall put ten thousand to flight** (Leviticus 26:7-8). God multiplies your strength. God caused armies of thousands to be defeated by godly men with only a few hundred on their side. When you have faith in God, the fight you are in is always fixed in your favor. You plus God, make a majority no matter how many oppose you.

God will deliver kings into your hands. *No man will be able to stand against you* because **God will put the dread and fear upon all those who oppose you** (Deuteronomy 7:24; 11:25). Joshua, a character who has a book that bears his name in the Bible, was a hero for God who defeated thirty-three kings. He experienced the reality of these verses as kings were delivered into his hands and all those who opposed him feared him. You can be a hero like Joshua.

Your enemies will flee from you seven ways. *One hero can chase a thousand and two heroes can put ten thousand to flight* (Deuteronomy 28:7; 32:30). When your enemies flee from you seven different ways you are invincible. The number seven stands for completion. Enemies who oppose you, an everyday hero, will be completely defeated.

As **God was with Joshua, He will be with you** if you believe (Joshua 1:5). As an everyday hero, you know that God is with you which strengthens your confidence and makes you a lethal weapon against evil. You are more than a conqueror through Christ Jesus. In Him, you cannot be defeated and you will always win.

You are fearless and know that **your enemies have been delivered into your hand** (Joshua 10:8; 21:44-45). You do not have to fear no matter who comes against you. God promises to deliver enemies into the hands of everyday heroes. It is important to know you belong to the Lord, Whom you serve. Trust God to deliver you out of any situation and He will.

An everyday hero **can take on larger enemies and win.** When the Lord is with you, it is like your enemy fighting one man (Joshua 23:9; Judges 6:16). You can take on enemies that are larger and stronger than you, and win. A true hero has God in him which makes him greater than anyone who is of this world. Your size is not the issue; **the size of your God is the important issue**.

God gives you supernatural ability to run against a troop

and leap over a wall (Psalm 18:2; Jeremiah 15:29). As God's hero, you have supernatural power to face challenges and win. Your belief in the Lord Jesus Christ makes everything that seems impossible possible. If an army opposes you or a wall stands before you, through God you can overcome and you are unstoppable.

> *Proverbs 21:22 says, "A wise man scales the city of the mighty, and brings down the trusted stronghold."*

You must believe you are invincible just like the Bible says you are. God makes you, His hero, tough and durable. The apostle Paul asks a question in Romans 8:31, "If God is for you who can be against you?" The answer to that question is no one. It is important to remember that you are only invincible by having a right relationship with Jesus Christ, the Lord of all, and walking with Him daily. Choose to be on God's side and on His team today because His team always wins.

DOUGLAS PYSZKA

Chapter 5

INTRODUCTION TO EVERYDAY HEROES IN THE BIBLE

The remaining pages consist of twelve men who were mighty heroes for God. They are identified by: their names; their mission; the heroic qualities they possessed; the magnitude of their tasks and the challenges they faced. These men are similar to you because they had strengths, faults, and made mistakes like you, yet they trusted God and rose up when it mattered most and they won. They are good examples to show you that you can recognize the God-given abilities you possess, use them to overcome life's challenges and win.

It is my desire for you to recognize your God-given abilities and develop the hero within you. I believe that all men can be everyday heroes for God by: having faith in Him, knowing Him, serving Him and following Him every day. Men face challenges, temptations and evil daily. Your super powers, your heroic qualities, were designed to face challenges of life and win. The information in this book is designed to help you, inspire you, and transform you into a godly hero as you study it.

I encourage you to recognize the heroic qualities that you have within you, activate them by faith and rise up to be more than a conqueror in Christ. You are destined to win and you can do all things through Christ who strengthens you. Be the hero God created you to be, **Be an everyday hero!**

Everyday Heroes of the Bible

- **Noah** – The persistent & faithful servant
- **Abraham** - The father of our faith
- **Joseph** - The dreamer who resisted temptation
- **Joshua** - The warrior servant
- **Moses** - The mighty deliverer

- **Mordecai** – The keeper of the gate of righteousness
- **Elisha** – A double portion carrier
- **Daniel** - The anointed statesman
- **Nehemiah** – The rebuilder of the wall of Jerusalem
- **Paul** – The Apostle of the Gentiles, kings and Israel
- **Peter** – The bold one with a great comeback
- **Timothy** – The faithful pastor

Chapter 6

NOAH AN EVERYDAY HERO FOR GOD

NOAH - Genesis

Name: Noah; repose; consolation; rest; relief (Hitchcock's Bible Names Dictionary)

Noah's Heroic Traits: Righteousness, Persistence, Faithfulness and Diligence

Mission: Noah was commissioned by God to build a floating fortress to house humans & animals 450 ft. long X 75 ft. wide X 45 ft. tall, all to save the world. A Nimitz aircraft carrier, a boat bigger than the ark, is about 1092 ft. in length and 257 ft. wide and carry 80-90 aircraft.   (Nimitz-class aircraft carrier (2015, September 20. In Wikipedia),

Noah's Heroic Qualities that Made Him an Everyday Hero:

- Radiant Righteousness
- Powerful Persistence
- Foundation of Faithfulness
- Diligent in his Doing

In the midst of darkness, Noah's life was radiant with righteousness. Everyone around Noah was wicked and evil. In all the wickedness, Noah found favor with God. He was able to communicate with God and God with Him. He had a relationship with God and God saw that Noah was righteous.

It was revealed to Noah that God was going to destroy the earth with a great flood because the earth was full of violence. God called Noah to an impossible task, to build a floating fortress and save the world. Noah would work at this assignment for many years. Year after year he had to maintain his faith in God and continue his work until it was finished. Noah saved himself and his family from destruction. He arose to the challenge he faced and became an everyday hero for God.

The Challenges Noah Faced

- He was surrounded by wickedness and evil people in the earth.
- He was misunderstood by most.
- He was unappreciated by the masses.
- He was ridiculed and mocked by the crowds.
- Noah was a minority with only his wife, his three sons and his three daughters-N- law.
- He also endured criticism of his call as the people would see Noah building this project.

The Magnitude of His Task

- God called Noah to be a hero and save the world.
- God would establish His covenant with Noah and his family.
- God told Noah that the earth would be destroyed and Noah was to build a giant floating fortress to house him, his family and representatives of all animals on the earth.
- This was an enormous building project that God asked Noah to do.
- Noah had to get building material, food for his family & animals, and complete the project.
- Noah had to follow God's plan wholeheartedly because His plan is always successful.

There are four heroic characteristics that stood out in Noah's life. These were his super powers that made him a hero for God. You may not be involved in a building project like building a giant ark, but you have a mission and face challenges in life just like Noah did. Learn how Noah used his super powers to be a champion so you can develop your own and be a champion too.

1.   Heroic Quality One - Noah was Righteous

Righteousness is a powerful heroic characteristic that causes you live right and act honorably according to God's divine law. Nelson's Bible dictionary defines righteousness this way:

> *"It is holy and upright living, in accordance with God's standard. The word righteousness comes from a root word that means, 'straightness.' It refers to a state that conforms to an authoritative standard. Righteousness is a moral concept. God's character is source of all righteousness."*

The Lord is perfect and just in all His ways. He is faithful and true and does what is right and fair (Deuteronomy 32:4). In a dark world, God needs men like you who are unashamed to do what is right every day. Righteousness strengthened Noah. He was set apart to be a godly hero; it put him in a position to receive God's plan and save his family from destruction.

The Bible teaches us: the word of the Lord is right; His work is done in truth and He loves righteousness and justice (Psalm 33:5). Righteousness and justice are the foundation of God's throne and He desires for His heroes to live righteous lives every day (Psalm 97:2).

Genesis 6:9 describes Noah's righteousness: He was a just man, perfect in his generations and he walked with God. Noah's righteousness enabled him to find God's favor. God sends His deliverance through righteousness.

Genesis 7:1 tells us, "God saw that Noah was righteous before Him in his generation." If you believe in Jesus, you are the righteousness of God in Christ Jesus through faith in Him. Although it was difficult, Noah remained righteous while there was so much wickedness around him. His righteousness motivated him to act honorably toward God. The people on the earth, at that time, were so wicked, that God decided to destroy them all except for Noah and his family. Only eight people trusted in the Lord at the time Noah lived. It is Faith in Jesus Christ that makes you righteous.

The Heroic Characteristic of Righteousness in Scripture

Looking at examples of righteous people may help you understand what righteousness is. You can make a positive impact in this world by living a righteous life. Being righteous is choosing to trust God wholeheartedly and live according to His divine laws.

Asa, a king of Judah, did what was good and right in the eyes of the LORD his God (2 Chron. 14:2). Only God can determine what is right , therefore righteousness is to abide by the standards that He has set. Not everyone does what is right in God's sight; Asa and Noah were righteous, and you can be too. Get on the right team, God's team, and He will make you righteous.

Hezekiah, another king of Judah, did what was good and right and true before the LORD his God (2 Chron. 31:20). Hezekiah took it further than Asa and added truth to his righteousness. Anyone can become righteous simply by having faith in God and trusting in Him wholeheartedly but no one can be righteous without God.

Zechariah and Elizabeth, parents of John the baptizer, were both righteous before God, walking in all the commandments and ordinances of the Lord, blameless (Luke 1:5-6). Righteousness empowered them to have a child when Elizabeth was barren and they were both well advanced in years. Righteousness is an important and super power to have.

You who follow after righteousness, you who seek the LORD: Look to the righteous examples that God has given you in His Word (Isaiah 51:1-2). Righteousness begins by knowing Jesus and it is worth pursuing. Abraham pursued it and attained it, by believing God (Romans 4:3). The only way you become righteous is the same way Abraham became righteous, by having faith in God. The Lord has called you in righteousness and He will hold your hand, helping you live it (Isaiah 42:6).

The righteousness of God is revealed from faith to faith; as it is written, "The just shall live by faith." (Romans 1:17). Live a righteous life by continuing to do what pleases God and do what He commands every day. Noah chose to live a life of faith and God considered him to be righteous. You can believe God, like Noah did and God will make you righteous also.

The God of your salvation answers you by awesome deeds in righteousness (Psalms 65:5).Righteousness comes from being confident in God which will result in you doing awesome things, like building an ark. The greatest example of righteousness is the Lord, Jesus who was righteous in all His ways (Psalm 119:137).

As a godly hero, you need the super power of righteousness in your life - so choose to trust God now and be an everyday hero who is right with Him.

2.   Heroic Quality Two - Noah was Persistent

Persistence is a powerful quality that enables a hero to overcome any challenge. A persistent person does not give up no matter how difficult life is. He overcomes tough challenges and achieves his God-given dreams. God is calling you to follow Him the rest of your life and complete the plan He has for you. Be persistent in following God: stay close to Him; keep His commands; Do what pleases Him. A persistent person always finds a way to get what he wants because he does not give up. Tap into the power of persistence and continue working until the job is done!

Noah's persistence made him a hero for God. He maintained his faith in God and kept his hope alive for many years. He was about five hundred years old when God spoke to him and he was six hundred years old when the flood waters came (Genesis 5:32; 7:6). Noah worked his assignment for a hundred years, longer than most people live today. A century was a long for him to: keep his faith strong; maintain a good attitude; do what God commanded him to do; refuse to quit when challenged and to finish well. Noah used his heroic quality of persistence very well and it saved his family.

Heroic Characteristic of Persistence in the Scriptures

Be steadfast, immovable, always abounding in the work of the Lord, knowing that your labor is not in vain in the Lord (1 Corinthians 15:58). These are three powerful descriptions of what it means to be persistent: steadfast, immovable and always abounding in the Lord's work. Noah exemplified these characteristics in his life. God has called you for greatness and to Himself. Follow through with your God-given assignment and do not quit until it is completed. Noah finished his work, Jesus finished His work, and you can finish what God calls you to do also (John 19:30).

Hezekiah became king of Judah at the age of twenty-five and he reigned for twenty-nine years in Jerusalem. He was a righteous reformer who fought against idolatry in his kingdom by trusting in the Lord God of Israel and holding fast to Him. He rooted out idolatry from his kingdom by removing the high places; breaking the sacred pillars and cutting down the wooden images. He followed God all his days (2 Kings 18:1-8). Persistence is holding fast to the Lord; refusing to quit; getting up every day and being a faithful worker, husband, father, son or friend.

Persistence is enduring to the end, even though many people may hate you (Matthew 10:22).

As a persistent person: be able to suffer and endure hardship for your path may not always be easy. When difficulty increases or a challenge rises up, do not quit; face them with the attitude that you win just by showing up. God provides you with sufficient strength to meet every difficult challenge.

Persistence holds steadfastly to the Lord's way and increases in strength (Job 17:9). Stay on the course the Lord has placed you on, even though you may be tempted to quit. Noah was probably tempted to be discouraged and to give up, but he kept doing what he was called to do, in spite of the ridicule, the mocking and the criticism he endured. He was a mighty hero.

Eternal life comes through patient continuance in doing what is right (Romans 2:7). Be patient and do not lose heart (Galatians 6:9). Noah had to be patient because it took a long time to complete his mission. He may have wondered if his building project was ever going to be finished. In spite of what Noah may have felt, He finished what he was called to do proving he was persistent.

The Lord Himself will teach and train you how to function in the super power of persistence. Knowing the character of Jesus will help you to continue in following His teaching (2 Timothy 3:14-15). God instructed Noah how to build the ark and make it float, and Noah followed God's master plan to the end. Together, they were a great success. With God, you win; without Him, you lose.

By refusing to quit and remaining consistent every day, you can be an everyday hero.

3.   Heroic Quality Three - Noah was Faithful

Faithfulness is a mighty heroic characteristic. A faithful hero is dependable, trustworthy and consistent in taking care of small and big assignments. Your faithfulness will be challenged every day. You must purpose in your heart to be faithful to God, your family, your employer, your friends and the promises you make. They are depending on you to be a faithful super hero.

Noah was faithful to do according to all that God commanded him (Genesis 6:22; 7:5). God spoke to Noah and told him to build an ark. Noah responded by doing what God said with all his heart, soul and strength. He did not deviate from God's plan, but gathered what he needed to build the boat and care for its passengers. Noah displayed the heroic characteristic of faithfulness by being dependable, trustworthy and consistent in building the ark. He worked on it for many years until it was completed. As you are faithful to God, you can be an everyday hero like Noah was.

The Heroic Characteristic of Faithfulness in Scripture

Know that the Lord your God is the Faithful God who keeps covenant and mercy for many generations (Deuteronomy 7:9). God keeps His Word and is trustworthy because faithfulness is His nature.

A faithful hero finishes what he starts and his work helps people for many generations. You must be faithful to love God and keep His commandments. Unfaithfulness is proof you lack love. The ark was a faith project which began and was completed by faith. Choose to be faithful today and finish what God assigns you to do.

Faithfulness transforms a servant into a ruler, who lacks no good thing (Matthew 24:45-46). God values and promotes faithfulness in His kingdom. As you are faithful to complete little tasks, God will make you responsible for bigger tasks. Joseph, another hero you will look at, was a faithful servant who was promoted to the second highest position in a foreign government. Joseph's faithfulness brought him increase and promotion.

A faithful hero increases in authority and responsibility (Luke 19:17-18). Faithfulness is proven in little assignments. If you handle little things well, your assignments increase through faithfulness. God was able to assign Noah the big task of building the ark, because he was faithful to maintain his relationship with God. God knew that Noah was faithful because he sought God when others did not. Noah was as obedient in building the ark, as he was in living for God. Noah used his super power of faithfulness to become extraordinary.

The Lord preserves the faithful like a shield defends a soldier (Psalms 31:23). Faithfulness is like a life preserver to a person in deep water that cannot swim. It will hold him up and prevent him from drowning. It was Noah's faithfulness that preserved him and his family from being destroyed by the flood. If you are faithful to God, He will preserve you also.

The Lord's faithfulness is great because His love prevents believers from perishing and His mercies never end (Lamentations 3:22-23). The greatest hero of all time, Jesus, is faithful and you should strive to be like Him. Everything God asks you to do requires faithfulness. Noah was faithful to God and God was faithful to Noah. Noah did not perish because he trusted in God's faithfulness.

Faithfulness means you are a man of your word and will stand by it until it is performed (Ezekiel 37:14). If God did not do what He said He would do, this universe would fall apart because it is upheld by His words. Noah did what God said and demonstrated His faithfulness to the Word of God.

4.   Heroic Quality Four - Noah was Diligent

As a hero, you must be a diligent doer and give your best every day. A diligent hero works hard, putting forth much effort. He pays careful attention to details and he does more than what he is required to do. Develop your diligence as Noah did.

Noah was diligent in his doing. He carried out God's will with the tenacity of a bulldog holding onto its favorite bone. He followed God's plan for building the ark just as God laid it out. He pleased God in what he did by doing a great job. Noah was a diligent doer of God's word which made him a hero. Develop the super power of diligence in your life and become an everyday hero.

The Heroic Characteristic of Diligence in Scripture

Follow God's commands diligently. Work hard and smart in God's kingdom (Ezra 7:23). Represent the Lord well by giving your best every day. Doing God's work and obeying Him should be your highest priority. Being a Christian is not for the fearful, the faint-hearted, the timid or the shy. It is for the bold believer who gives his best to God.

Diligence increases wealth (Proverbs 10:4). Noah exercised due diligence in building the ark and preparing for its voyage. The ark that Noah and his family built withstood the most intense flooding the world has ever seen. His diligence produced great results. It was God's plan and Noah's diligence that provided all in the ark with plenty, lacking no good thing (Proverbs 21:5). Develop your super power of diligence.

A diligent hero fights to the end without being sluggish. You can imitate other godly heroes who inherited what God promised through faith and patience (Hebrews 6:11-12). Develop a habit of finishing what you start, like reading a book from beginning to end. The assignments that God will give you require you to be diligent. God is worthy of your best effort. Perhaps you will be inspired by Noah's diligence.

As a diligent hero, you will act on God's Word even when you do not feel like it. The Lord asked Peter to cast his nets in the water. Peter did not want to do what Jesus said because he had done that all night and caught nothing. Peter disregarded how he felt and cast his net in and caught an amazing bunch of fish (Luke 5:5).

God's word produces much better results than your physical toil. There may have been times when Noah wanted to quit because his task seemed so great but he remained diligent and built the ark which saved him, his family and humanity. Whatever God calls you to do, do it diligently and God will bless you.

The super hero power of diligence should increase, abound, and become stronger every day (2 Corinthians 8:7). Continue to fine tune your diligence and look for opportunities to help others, and you will experience the power of diligence.

To help you understand Noah's four heroic characteristics, there are some questions for you to consider. Take your time and answer them sincerely. Take notice of where you can improve and decide to be better. Ask God to help you be an everyday hero. ☐

Questions to Consider for Your Personal Growth in Becoming an Everyday Hero like Noah

1.   What project, assignment or task that God has given you to do has been left unfinished or incomplete?

2.   What would it take for you to finish that project, assignment or task you left unfinished?

3.   What obstacles, challenges and difficulties are hindering you from completing your assignment?

4.   In the next 15-30 days, what will you do differently to be faithful in the little things?

5.   Are you confident that you can hear God's voice, receive His revelations and instructions?

6.   How does God Speak to you?

7.   How can you find favor with God? (See Hebrews 4)

8.   What Scripture(s) stood out to you the most about the heroic qualities that Noah displayed? How will you apply those to your life?

9.   Choose three Scriptures from this lesson and memorize them.

Chapter 7

ABRAHAM AN EVERYDAY HERO FOR GOD

ABRAHAM - Genesis

Name: ABRAM high father; Abraham father of a great multitude (Hitchcock's Bible Names Dictionary), AY bruh ham] (father of a multitude); originally Abram (exalted father) - the first great Patriarch of ancient Israel and a primary model of faithfulness for Christianity. (Nelson's Illustrated Bible Dictionary).

Abraham's Heroic Traits: Obedience, Willingness, Faith, Worship

Mission: He was called by God to be a father of a multitude, to establish and build a new nation, and become a father of a new natural and spiritual race. He became the leader of a great spiritual army.

Abraham's Heroic Qualities that Made Him an Everyday Hero

- Outstanding Obedience
- Working Willingness to Do, Go and Be what God said
- Firm Faith
- Diligent Worshiper

The Challenges Abraham Faced

- He was called to be a father of many nations when he had no children.
- He had to leave all that he was familiar with and pioneer a new race of people.
- He had to wander through unknown territory.
- He had only the possessions that he could carry.
- He was going to do something that had not been done before.
- He was at an age when most people are retired at today.

The Magnitude of Abraham's Task

- God called Abraham to be a hero and father nations when he had no children.
- Sarai was barren when she was and now that season had passed.
- Abraham had to change his location several times.
- God chose to create a new nation with Abraham not someone else.
- Abram and Sarah were in their seventies when God spoke to him.

Before his name was changed, Abraham was known as Abram. God called Abraham to pioneer a new race of people. In order to do that, he had to separate himself from his old associations and go forth to a place that God would show him. God promised him divine favor, a great posterity, and that he would become a blessing to all the families of the earth. Abraham obeyed God's call to become the leader of the innumerable pilgrims who look for a city whose architect and builder is God (Hebrews 11:8-10).

God spoke to Abraham in Genesis and told him to leave his country, his family and his father's house (Genesis 12:1-3). God would show Abraham where to go as he went on his way. God wants to see if you will obey Him in taking step one before He reveals step two to you. Abraham's reward for obeying the Lord's command was to be famous, wealthy and become a great nation. This was an amazing promise since Abraham did not have any children at this point in his life. How does one man become a great nation? How does a man who is very old become a father? That man hears God's voice, obeys what He says wholeheartedly, acts on God's Words and God does the miraculous.

Abraham received instructions from headquarters, which he had to obey. To disregard God's instructions is to miss out on His tremendous blessings. Abraham's obedience to God led him to be richly rewarded. The magnitude of the rewards that God gives is in proportion to the obedience of His servants. Abraham obeyed God and departed as the Lord had spoken to him (Genesis 12:4). He simply took God at His word and did what the Lord commanded him to do.

There are four heroic characteristics that made Abraham a godly hero. You may possess similar heroic qualities as Abraham had or your heroic qualities may be different. Recognize your God-given qualities and use them to be an everyday hero.

1. Heroic Quality One - Abraham had Outstanding Obedience

Nelson's Bible Dictionary defines obedience this way: "Obedience is carrying out the word and will of another person, especially the will of God. In both the Old and New Testaments the word *obey* is related to the idea of hearing. Obedience is a positive, active response to what a person hears. God summons people to active obedience to His revelation. Man's failure to obey God results in judgment." (Nelson's Illustrated Bible Dictionary Ibid.)

The Lord spoke to Abraham. He instructed him about his assignment, and promised to reward and bless him for his obedience. Abraham immediately began to do all the Lord spoke to him and venture into the unknown (Genesis 12:4).

Exodus 19:4-6 says, "If you will indeed obey God's voice and keep His covenant, He will consider you His special treasure. You will be a kingdom of priests and a holy nation." This passage of Scripture expresses God's heart toward those that **have outstanding obedience** like Abraham had. God treasured Abraham's obedience. Through his obedience to God, Abraham became a great nation. As you are obedient to God, you will accomplish great things too.

Obedience is important to God and He values it more than a sacrificial offering given to Him. God considers someone who is disobedient to be a stubborn rebel (1 Samuel 15:22-23). To reject what God said is to reject God Himself. There are severe consequences when a person rejects God's Word.

Abraham received God's Word and respected it by doing what God said. Honor the Lord by obeying His Word to you. Your obedience to God every day makes you a godly hero.

Ways Abraham Obeyed God

Abraham obeyed God in avoiding strife and loving people. Strife allows every other evil work to come in and destroy a good relationship. In Genesis Ch. 13, Abraham & Lot increased so much, that the land was not able to support them both. Their herdsmen were in strife, arguing with each about the insufficiency. Abraham stopped strife from entering his heart and demonstrated that he obeyed God. God is against strife and you should be too. Abraham allowed Lot, his nephew, to choose where he would dwell and Abraham promised to go the opposite direction.

Abraham revealed his humility by allowing Lot to choose where to go. He could have told Lot where to go. Instead, he trusted in the Lord which turned out much better for him. You will get better results by trusting God also. Abraham resembled God's nature and heart by stopping strife swiftly.

Abraham obeyed God in giving. In Genesis Ch. 14, Lot was taken captive by four kings and their armies. Abraham armed his servants to rescue his nephew, Lot. Abraham's rescue squad defeated the larger armies; rescued Lot; and recovered all the goods that were taken.

After the great victory, Abraham met Melchizedek, king of Salem, and gave him a tenth of all the spoil. Abraham did not have a written law telling him to give this amount, but Abraham knew something about God that inspired him to give. Abraham honored and obeyed God in giving a tenth to His High Priest and God blessed him mightily. Be obedient to God with your finances and He will bless you like He blessed Abraham. Be willing to honor God with your substance and He will honor you (Proverbs 3:9-10)

Abraham obeyed God in keeping His covenant. In Genesis 17, God made a covenant with Abraham to walk before Him, be blameless and receive a new name. Abraham followed God's instruction and he circumcised every male in his household along with himself. God honors obedience.

Abraham and Sarah had a son, Isaac, when it was physically impossible for them to have a child after obeying God's covenant a few years. They were past the age of when their bodies could produce and carry offspring. Yet God worked a miracle. Abraham circumcised his son Isaac when he was eight days old, as God had commanded him (Genesis 21:4). **Abraham showed heroic obedience**.

Abraham obeyed God in offering Isaac to God. In Genesis Ch. 22, God asked Abraham to sacrifice his son Isaac. Abraham readily and quickly obeyed the Lord, got up early and set out to go where God would lead him. He was willing and obedient to carry out God's command exactly as it was spoken to him and follow God's command explicitly. If God asked you to sacrifice something you greatly valued, would you obey? If you obeyed God like Abraham you would be an everyday hero.

Heroic Characteristic of Obedience in Scripture

Obedience is an important heroic quality. Ultimately, you should **obey God's commands** because they are commands, not suggestions. Obedience to authority reveals what kind of man you are. You can only exercise authority after obeying authority. Be a man who respects authority and God will do great things through you.

Obedience is observing, keeping and walking in God's commands (Leviticus 18:4).Obedience to God gives and maintains life while disobedience to Him causes death. As a hero, do what God commands you to do. Eliminate options on the right and left by looking straight ahead at the Lord. Live as God commands you to live and it will be well with you for a long time (Deuteronomy 5:32-33; 6:1). Obeying God's Word enables you to possess what God promised you.

Obedience means you love the Lord your God and keep His

word always (Deuteronomy 11:1).Your obedience to God is proof you love Him. Do not add or subtract anything to what God said because it is good on its own, it is eternal and forever settled (Deuteronomy 12:32).

The quicker you learn to discern God's voice and how He speaks to you, the easier it is to obey Him (Deuteronomy 27:10). **Obedience to God is a daily requirement for success in life**. Train yourself to be quick to obey and choose to be loyal to God. Your loyalty to God produces a heavenly royalty (1 Kings 8:61)

God will remember you and fulfill His promises to you, as you obey Him (Psalms 105:42-45). God never forgets His promises. He always does what He says. Obedience to God brings good things to you. Obey God above men and make it your highest priority in life (Acts 5:29). Develop your super hero power of obedience to God daily and become an everyday hero.

2. Heroic Quality Two – Abraham was Willing to Do, Go and Be what God Said

Willingness combined with obedience are important heroic qualities. Willingness is: an attitude of your heart; it compels you to do what God wants; it aligns you to do His will above anything else. To receive the best that God offers you, be willing and obedient to Him and do things His way. Allow God to lead, guide and direct your life and He will bring you into greatness.

Abraham was a person who loved God and was willing to go where God sent him. When God asked him to leave, he left willingly (Genesis. 12:4; 26:5; Hebrews 11:8; Acts 7:4-8).

God called Abraham to be a father of many nations and He became that father through his **willingness to do, go and be what God said**. Abraham overcame the physical challenge of his age supernaturally. **He eagerly and enthusiastically obeyed God's commands**. Abraham gave to God whatever He asked for; he did whatever God said to do; he went wherever God led him to go and he heeded all that God said. Abraham had faults and made mistakes but he willingly corrected his ways when he was confronted by God (Genesis 13:17-18; 14:20; 15:6; 17:10-14; 23-27; Ch. 18; Ch. 22). His willingness made him an everyday hero and if you are willing, you can be a hero too.

Heroic Characteristic of Willingness in Scripture

How can you become more willing? Willingness and obedience are rewarded and disobedience is punished (Isaiah 1:19-20). These two qualities work together like a driver and a car. A car does not move on its own because it needs a driver to direct it. **Willingness is agreeing that God's Word is true and obedience is the action taken to fulfill it.** Exercise the super power of willingness to be a godly hero.

Here are some ways that you can test your willingness. Answer these questions truthfully in your heart and see how willing you are. Look up the Scriptures that are listed for a deeper meaning and make adjustments the Lord leads you to make.

Do you offer yourself to the leaders that God has placed in your life and are you available to serve and follow them? (Judges 5:2).

How willing are you to give money to God when given the opportunity? (Exodus 35:5; 21).

Do you desire to hear God's voice and do what He tells you? (1 Samuel 3:10).

How do your mind and heart agree with God's plan for your life?

Are you willing to use your skill and yield to the leader in charge? (1 Chronicles 28:21).

You need a loyal heart and a willing mind to serve God (1 Chronicles 28:9-10). God will test how willing you are (1 Chronicles 29:17). God will reward your willingness (1 Corinthians 9:16-18).

As an everyday hero, you volunteer to do whatever the Lord asks of you. He always allows you to choose. The attitude of your heart is revealed by how you respond to opportunities to help others (Philemon 1:14). Be a godly hero every day by willing to do what God wants you to do.

3. Heroic Quality Three – Abraham Had a Firm Faith in God

As a godly hero, you need to have a firm faith in God, a faith that is strong, endures long and refuses to quit. God must be the object and source of your faith. The Word of God is the only spring that pure faith flows from. You can believe God because: He is true; He cannot lie; He does not change; and His Word endures forever. Faith is simply hearing what God says and acting it out. A phrase that sums up Abraham's faith is found in Genesis 12:4, *"Abram departed as the LORD had spoken to him."*

God revealed to Abraham what He had planned for him. Abraham responded by doing what God said, demonstrating the genuineness of his faith (Genesis 12:1-4). His firm faith in God made him righteous before God (Genesis 15:6; Romans 4:3-9; 20-25; Galatians 3:6-14; Hebrews 11:8; James 2:23).

Abraham did not let anything interfere with his faith. When strife sprung up between Abraham and Lot, Abraham stopped it so it would not hinder his faith (Genesis 13:8-18). Abraham kept his faith strong by not considering his body, which was past the age of producing offspring or Sarah's womb, which was dead (Romans 4:19). Instead, he considered God's nature, character and His promise to be the things he focused on.

Firm faith trusts God wholeheartedly. God agreed with how Abraham dealt with strife and rewarded him by giving him all the land he could see in every direction. Abraham's firm faith produced lasting results and made him a godly hero. Strengthen your faith in God and be an everyday hero.

Abraham believed God. Even though **there were times when Abraham doubted what God promised** him, **He kept his faith in God**. At one point, Abraham was more focused on his childlessness then he was on God's promise. He was looking to what he did not have, instead of looking at what God promised him. The Lord strengthened Abraham's faith with a vision of the stars. God told Abraham to look at the stars and said that his descendants would be as numerous as them (Genesis 15:4-7). God will address your doubts and encourage you in ways to believe what He spoke to you. If you have any doubts about God, do not quit, but seek Him, and you will find Him and He will give you the answers you seek.

After seeing the stars and being reassured of what God promised, Abraham **believed God**. In exercising firm faith in God, Abraham became righteous. His relationship with God was solidified and strengthened.

Abraham demonstrated **firm faith in God in willingly offering to sacrifice his son Isaac**. God asked Abraham to offer his son as a sacrifice to the Lord on an altar. Abraham was fully persuaded of the truth, if Isaac died, he would be resurrected. That is firm faith

Abraham did not flinch when God requested Isaac as be offered, but he confidently obeyed Him. The Lord knew that Abraham was trustworthy and He tested him and he passed. Firm faith is willing to sacrifice anything to the Lord because it is convinced that it will produce an eternal reward. Abraham's faith made him a hero for God. You can be a godly hero also with firm faith in God (Genesis Ch. 22).

Other Examples of Firm Faith

- A Roman centurion's firm faith brought healing to his servant (Matthew 8:10).
- A woman's firm faith delivered her daughter from demonic possession (Matthew 15:28).
- Nathaniel's firm faith increased his spiritual vision and caused him heavenly things (John 1:51).
- A woman's firm faith caused her to be healed from twelve years of hemorrhaging (Mark 5:34).
- Bartimaeus' great faith opened his blind eyes (Mark 10:52).
- The leper's firm faith made him whole and completely free from leprosy (Luke 17:19)

4. Heroic Quality Four – Abraham was a Diligent Worshiper

A godly hero is a worshiper of God. To worship God is to: recognize Him and His divine qualities; honor Him for what He has done; direct your praise to Him and give Him thanks. God is worthy of your worship and His presence inhabits your praise of Him and He will shower you with His power making you into a mighty hero.

Wherever Abraham dwelt, he built an altar to worship God. Worship was an important part of his daily life. Only those who truly love God develop a worshipful lifestyle. You must set aside a time and a place to worship God every day. In your place of worship, make an appointment with God to read His word, meditate in it, pray to Him and rejoice in Him.

The altar was the place where Abraham acknowledged God as the source of all good things in his life. There, he demonstrated his love for God and offered sacrificial gifts to Him. Abraham would call on the name of the Lord and fellowship with Him at the altar (Genesis 13:3-4; 18; 17:1-8; 22:9-12)

God met with Abraham at the altar; He revealed Himself to him; He poured out blessings upon him. You will experience the same things in your own life as you follow Abraham's example in worshiping God. His worship to God made him a strong hero. You can worship God and be an everyday hero also (Exodus 17:15-16; 20:23-26; 24:4-8).

Heroic Characteristic of Worship in Scripture

Abraham described his experience in offering Isaac as worship to God (Genesis 22:4-5). There is only one person that is worthy of your exclusive worship, God. Worshiping God takes guts and shows your commitment . God works mightily through those who worship Him. God invites and welcomes you to worship Him (Exodus 34:14-17).

A hero worships God in his giving and he gives his best to help others. He brings his ten percent into God's house to support His work: He gives offerings freely, as needs arise, and he helps the poor as he can. A generous giver rejoices at every opportunity to give. Giving finances to God is one way to you can worship him (Deuteronomy 26:10-12; 1 Chronicles16:29).

God can be worshiped anywhere but He set up His church to be a special place of worship (Psalms 5:7-8). God's church is the people who come together in the name of Jesus, not the building where they meet. Special things take place where God's church worships Him in Spirit and Truth. Worship is giving God what He is due (Psalms 29:2). Every Biblical hero worshiped God.

Worship is how you express to God what you think, feel and know about Him. You can express how you feel about God in many ways such as: you can worship Him in different positions; you can worship with your voice; you can act on His Word; you can speak words and sing songs. God will also speak to you as you worship Him (Psalm 95:6-8; 96:9).

God provides you with two powerful tools, His Word and His Spirit, to help you be the heroic worshiper He created you to be. True worship empowers every hero. Choose to worship God today and take your place as a godly hero (John 4:22-24).

To help you understand these four heroic characteristics that made Abraham a hero, there are some questions for you to consider. Take your time and answer these sincerely. Strive to be the best you can be and decide to develop your own heroic qualities. Ask God to help you be an everyday hero.

Questions to consider for your personal growth in becoming an everyday hero like Abraham

1. Has God asked you to do something that was never done before?

2. How willing are you to step out from something that is comfortable to something that is difficult and uncomfortable?

3. When the Lord speaks to you, how long does it take you to obey His instruction?

4. Do you need extra proof from God to follow through with what He has spoken to you?

5. Would you be able to sacrifice someone or something that you treasure greatly?

6. What things have you sacrificed to obey God?

7. Would you be willing to give everything to God if He asked for it?

8. Do you do what God says or do you add things to what He says?

9. Does what you believe produce the results you expect or desire?

10. What things have helped you confront and overcome doubts you may have had?

11. How often do you meet with God? What are some things you discuss?

12. Do you find it easy or difficult to enter into God's presence? What are some things you do that causes you to be very aware of God's presence and does it seem like it takes a long time for you to get in God's presence?

Chapter 8

JOSEPH AN EVERYDAY HERO FOR GOD

JOSEPH - Genesis

Name: Increase; addition   (from Hitchcock's Bible Names Dictionary) [JOE zeph] (May God add).

Mission: His mission was to save his people from destruction & famine. God placed him in Egypt, at the right time and in the right position, to save Israel and other nations. Joseph testified that God sent him to preserve a future for Israel (Genesis 45:5-8)

Joseph's Heroic Traits: Administration, Faithfulness, Integrity, Dream Interpretation

Joseph's Heroic Qualities That Made Him an Everyday Hero:

- Excellent administration & management abilities
- Fruitful & productive faithfulness
- Impeccable integrity
- Divine dream interpreter

The Challenges Joseph Faced

- He was eleventh of twelve children.
- His brothers hated him and he had family strife & tension.
- He was sold into slavery by his brothers.
- His father, Jacob, thought that Joseph was dead.
- People who were close to Joseph, lied about him and falsely accused him of things.
- How would Joseph get to the right place to save Israel?

The Magnitude of Joseph's Task

- Joseph saw his family bowing down to him in the future but did not know how it would happen.
- He would be taken to a foreign country as a teen to be there to save his people.
- How could a slave save others when he himself is captive?
- Joseph would face many setbacks and challenges that he would have to overcome.
- There was only one person in Egypt whom God would use to interpret Pharaoh's dreams.

There are four heroic characteristics that made Joseph a hero for God: administration, integrity, faithfulness and dream interpretation. Your heroic characteristics may be similar to Joseph's; or yours may differ from his. Take time to develop your God-given abilities to be an everyday hero.

Joseph's parents were Jacob & Rachel. Jacob had four wives but he loved Rachel the most. They were unable to have children for many years. Finally, Rachel conceived and gave birth to Joseph. Because Joseph was born to Jacob when he was older, he loved Joseph very much. Jacob made Joseph a multicolored tunic or coat, signifying God's favor on Joseph. The favoritism that Jacob showed to Joseph made his brothers jealous, and they hated Joseph because he was treated better than they were.

God began to develop Joseph's heroic qualities from the time he was born. Jacob, Joseph's father, assigned Joseph to watch his brothers and report what they were doing (Genesis 37:2; 12-16). Joseph sharpened his administrative and managerial skills as he observed his brother's work and reported what he saw to his father. Jacob trusted Joseph with this important task which helped developed his heroic skills. In every challenge Joseph faced, his heroic qualities helped him win.

God favors His heroes which stirs envy and jealousy in hearts of people who do not understand God's ways. God had a plan for Joseph and He moved Him where He wanted him to be and set him for His own purposes. God created you on purpose and you must follow His plan for your life. To become a hero for God you must discover your purpose, follow it and fulfill it. You may not like where are, but do what you were created to do here. Begin now to be God's hero.

In spite of all the difficulties he faced, Joseph maintained a good attitude and remained faithful to Lord. Just like you, he was tempted to be frustrated and may have wanted to give up, but he rose to meet his challenges heroically and won. Joseph was an effective worker; he succeeded at whatever he did; he made his bosses very profitable. Although Joseph was a slave, he did not have a slave mentality. He worked like he owned the company and made much money.

1. Heroic Quality One – Joseph, Excelled in Administration and Increased in Everything

An administrator manages groups of people large or small. God gives an administrator his ability.

God needs heroes to take the lead and achieve success for Him. A hero needs to manage all of his resources well: his skill, money, time, projects and people. Become a good manager who is diligent and who knows the condition of his resources (Proverbs 27:23-24).

Jacob was in the livestock business and managed herds and flocks of animals. Joseph managed his brothers and reported their work results to his father every day. Joseph developed his administrative skills early in life. He knew what was needed to make a job profitable. Joseph's reports must have been truthful and accurate in order for Jacob to trust Joseph to do this. He was developing in his heroic skills (Genesis 37:2; 12-17).

With the heroic quality of administration, you learn that faithfulness in little things lead to bigger things. Follow Joseph's example in being a good manager. God will test you to see if He can trust you. As a manager, be excellent in all you do.

Joseph's administrative skills set him apart from his brothers.

His brothers spent their time in the field, with the flocks, while Joseph spent time with his father at home. Joseph's siblings wore shepherds clothes while he wore a multi-colored tunic. Joseph used the skills he developed at home when he went to Egypt.

In Genesis 39, Joseph ended up in Egypt. His own brothers sold him as a slave to a group of merchants who then sold him to Potiphar in Egypt. Joseph worked for Potiphar, an Egyptian, the captain of the king's guard. God gave Joseph favor, which made him so successful, his master promoted him to a high position. Joseph could be a CEO in any major corporation today and that company would be profitable because Joseph would be running it.

Joseph's success did not come without challenges. Joseph was sentenced to prison because he was falsely accused by Potiphar's wife of making advances towards her. Actually, she tried to seduce Joseph but he had such a strong character, he resisted the temptation to sleep with her and fled the scene, leaving his coat behind.

After being in prison for a while Joseph was promoted to manage other prisoners. God always causes his heroes to rise to the top no matter what they face. Because Joseph was a hero, he was put in charge wherever he ended up. He even helped other prisoners by interpreting their dreams accurately (Genesis 39:21-23).

Joseph's heroic quality of administration caused him to prosper as a slave, a prisoner and a forgotten dream interpreter. God's power worked in Joseph to do amazing things in his life and enabled him to be a top notch administrator. You can be an everyday hero by learning how manage your resources well like Joseph did.

Heroic Characteristic of Administration in Scripture

Be a faithful and wise supervisor, do what God says and follow His plan till He returns (Luke 12:42-44). Continue to sharpen your skills and influence more people by using the talents God gave you. Do not hide your talents but use them to do God's work

(Matthew 25:20-23).

Isaac was a good manager because he obeyed God and followed His instruction to stay and sow where God instructed him. He became so wealthy that his wealth exceeded king Abimelech's who ruled where Isaac lived. The king was so jealous of Isaac's wealth that he told him to leave his territory. That is a super hero administrator (Genesis 26:12-16).

David was a mighty warrior, a good administrator and a king who used his skills to increase wherever he went and God was with him. **He acted wisely in all his ways** and Israel and Judah loved him (1 Samuel 16:18; 18:14-16). **A good administrator is productive and profitable in all seasons** because he receives strength from God and he is not dismayed or fearful. Being a good manager is to take good care of what God has given you and seek to honor God in whatever you do. Start by influencing your family to follow God and keep all His ways. If you have children, train them to serve and follow the Lord God (Psalm 1:3; Isaiah 41:10; Proverbs 27:18; Genesis 18:19).

People are the most valuable resource a manager has. As a godly hero, learn how to work with people. Your success depends upon them, so recognize those who help you and honor those in authority over you. Joseph did this in Potiphar's house (1 Thessalonians 5:12-15).

Learn from the good leaders who influence you and follow the examples of people who manage well what God gave them. **The results you get from the work you do define your skill as a manager**. A good manager increases profit and a poor manager diminishes profit. Does what you manage increase or decrease? (Hebrews 13:7-9; Genesis 30:27-30).

The **keys to being a successful manager** for the Lord are: be strong and courageous; obey God's and speak God's Words; meditate in God's Word to get it in you; do what God says wholeheartedly (Joshua 1:7-9).

As a leader you must be fearless and avoid being discouraged. God will help you succeed and those who oppose

God will not share in the goodness that He gives to you (1 Chronicles 22:13; Nehemiah 2:20).

Joseph was a fearless leader because he never stopped trusting God and helping people whether he was in Potiphar's house, the prison or the palace. Wherever he went, he administered his God-given abilities to increase the people he worked for. Develop your administrative skills and you can be a godly hero.

2. **Heroic Quality Two – Joseph was Fruitful, Faithful & Productive**

Joseph was a successful man in whatever he ventured into. Wherever he was, increase occurred. He lived up to his name which means, *"May God add or increase."* **An important key to Joseph's fruitfulness and productivity was his faithfulness to God and His plan**. With the super power of faithfulness Joseph became a godly hero.

Joseph was faithful to follow God's principles daily. Faithfulness is performing small tasks well over a period of time. It is a quality that God admires and looks for in individuals.

Here are some ways that Joseph was faithful: he honored his father by obeying his instructions; he honored the Lord with a good attitude when bad things happened and he followed his dream even though he may not have understood it until later in his life (Genesis 37:2-16; 21-36; 39:1-6; 20).

Joseph worked as if he was working for the Lord even though he worked for an Egyptian. He faithfully served Potiphar and made him profitable. Joseph followed God's commands by not yielding to sin (Genesis 39:2-6; 9-12).

Even when put in prison, Joseph was given responsibility to oversee other prisoners. Joseph was very humble as he acknowledged God in all things and did not trust in nor promote himself. He used his God-given abilities to help people. He continued to be faithful even when people failed to acknowledge him or his work (Genesis 39:21-23; 40:8; 12-15; 23-41:1; 33-41).

Joseph used his super hero qualities to save Egypt and Israel by interpreting dreams, following God's plan in setting aside grain when it was in abundance and forgiving his brothers for the evil they did (Genesis 41:48-49; 45:3-8; 19-21).

Heroic Characteristic of Faithfulness in Scripture

God considered Moses to be a faithful worker in His kingdom and spoke to him face to face (Numbers 12:6-8).

As a faithful hero for God, know what is in God's heart and mind, by having an active relationship with Him and doing what He commands (1 Samuel 2:35). Faithfulness begins in your heart and works its way out into all that you do and how you live (Nehemiah 9:8).

God watches faithfulness closely, favors it, strengthens it and rewards it. As a faithful hero, you will be blessed abundantly by God. God abides with the faithful (Psalm 31:23-24; 101:6-7; Proverbs 28:20).

Your faithfulness is proven with little responsibilities. You may be instructed to begin work at a certain time. If you follow that instruction faithfully, you build trust, prove your dependability and may be promoted. Be faithful to follow and serve the Lord. Complete little instructions well to get more important assignments (Luke 16:9-12; Hebrews 3:1-2). Faithfulness is a powerful super hero quality that does great things for God.

3. Heroic Quality Three – Joseph had Impeccable Integrity

Christian character is defined as the force of a man's moral personality, as modified and developed by the work of God's Holy Spirit. God's word is the standard upon which good character is based. Good moral character is godly integrity and it is a powerful heroic characteristic which God values greatly.

The way you live and what your life reveals your character. Good character comes from knowing the Lord and doing what He says. The more you know about Him and obey Him, the more you will resemble Him and reflect His nature. Jesus had such good character that Pontius Pilate, the Roman ruler, could find no fault in Him. Follow Jesus' example and character.

Joseph developed his relationship with God from seeing and hearing his father, Jacob, live for God. **When Joseph faced challenges, he adhered to the values he believed in and exercised good character**. People who were around Joseph saw that he was a person with strong moral character to make good decisions. A man of character adheres to proven principles at all times and is consistent.

Joseph's biggest temptation came when Potiphar's wife tried to seduce him. Joseph was a handsome man, with authority and responsibility in Potiphar's house. Mrs. Potiphar was attracted to Joseph and tried several times to seduce him. **Joseph's character and integrity protected him from sin and kept his relationship with God intact**. Joseph's integrity is described in the following Scriptures.

Genesis 39:6-10 says, "Now Joseph was handsome in form and appearance. 7 And it came to pass after these things that his master's wife cast longing eyes on Joseph, and she said, "Lie with me." 8 But he refused and said to his master's wife, "Look, my master does not know what is with me in the house, and he has committed all that he has to my hand. 9 There is no one greater in this house than I, nor has he kept back anything from me but you, because you are his wife. How then can I do this great wickedness, and sin against God?" 10 So it was, as she spoke to Joseph day by day, that he did not heed her, to lie with her or to be with her." NKJV

What kind of woman was Mrs. Potiphar? She was willing to

sleep with a man that was not her husband. She was a wicked and deceitful woman because she created an atmosphere where no one was in her house but her and Joseph. A woman like Potiphar's wife will destroy your integrity and your life. Joseph did the right thing when it mattered most and protected his integrity.

Consider Joseph's integrity. Joseph refused his master's wife's advances. He spoke openly of the trust that Potiphar had in him and in the position he held. Joseph honored his master, even though he could have gotten away with this indiscretion and sin because of the position he held and the authority he had. Joseph maintained his integrity with God and Potiphar.

Joseph asked this question, "How then can I do this great wickedness, and sin against God?" He recognized that sin is against God. He called what his master's wife wanted to do *great wickedness*. She persisted to seduce Joseph and he resisted her advances for **many days**. A person of integrity is consistent in resisting temptation over a period of time. This was a spiritual fight that Joseph had to win in his heart. He had to cling to God and abhor evil. He was a hero for his strong integrity.

When this temptation reached its' peak, Joseph ran away. People of integrity will not compromise their character or allow themselves to be stained with sin. There may be times when you simply have to leave a situation to protect your integrity. In fleeing temptation, your enemy, the devil, will try to destroy your name and your character. If you honor God and protect your integrity, He will protect you and make you a victorious super hero.

Mrs. Potiphar lied about what happened to her. If she could not have Joseph, she would ruin his reputation. She falsely accused Joseph of trying to make an advance on her. As her husband heard what his wife said, he became very angry. He put Joseph in prison, but because of his integrity, God was with Joseph and he prospered in prison (Genesis 29:17-23).

God's presence was with Joseph and He rewarded him for his integrity. Even if no person was around to accuse Joseph, God would see, hear and know what happened. God sees what you do and hears what you say; so be a person of strong moral character and you will be an everyday hero for God.

God rewarded and promoted Joseph for being a person of integrity and having impeccable character. This result could not have happened if Joseph would have compromised his integrity.

Heroic Characteristics of Character & Integrity in Scripture

Good moral character reflects God's nature and it is profitable to you. Your character flows from your relationship with Christ and is who you are and what you do every day. If you know Christ, your character should be stronger than someone who does not know Christ (1 Timothy 4:8).

Integrity comes from wholeheartedly trusting in God and having a good conscience. A good conscience comes from living by God's standards found in His Word. Developing your character is a worthy pursuit. The way you develop your character is: Speak God's Word; meditate on Scriptures daily and obey all that God commands   (1 Timothy 1:19; 3:1-7; 6:11-14; Titus 2:7; Joshua 1:8).

As a godly hero, your integrity positively influences people and gives them an example they can follow.

Being a man with godly character will lead you to the top and help you prosper and succeed as it did for men in the Bible like *Daniel, Mordecai and Jehoshaphat* (1 Timothy 4:12-16).

A lack of character leads to self-destruction (1 Samuel 2:27-36). Choose to be a godly hero by keeping your integrity strong and refuse to compromise what you know is right.

4. **Heroic Quality Four – Joseph was a Divine Dream Interpreter.**

A dream is a state of mind in which images, thoughts, and impressions pass through the mind of a person who is sleeping. Dreams have had a prominent place in the religious literature of ancient peoples. In ancient times, dreams-especially those

*of kings and priests-were thought to convey
messages from God   (from Nelson's Illustrated
Bible Dictionary IBID)*

God spoke to Joseph through a dream at an early age and showed him a picture of what would happen later in his life. God did not show Joseph how that dream would be fulfilled, he just gave him a glimpse of the future. Joseph's dreams revealed his family would bow down to him. When Joseph shared his dreams with his brothers, they did not like the thought of Joseph reigning over them.

Jacob favored Joseph above his eleven brothers, and gave Joseph a coat of many colors representing God's anointing on his life (Genesis 37:3-11). God distinguishes people for their divine assignments by setting them apart from others and giving them God-given abilities. Joseph's coat represented his God-given abilities or super powers to administrate, lead, rule and interpret dreams. Dreams from God are often in color. This coat was similar to the capes that Batman and Superman wear. Heroes need cool costumes.

God used the tool of interpreting dreams to get Joseph where he needed to be. Joseph's brothers hated him for his dreams and the words he spoke. What God uses to distinguish you, your enemy will use to hate you and despise you.

When Joseph was in prison, he correctly interpreted two dreams of inmates. Joseph acknowledged God as the One who reveals the meaning of dreams (Genesis 40:8). He wanted those inmates to remember him and perhaps he would be released from prison. One of the prisoners, the royal baker, was executed and the other , the royal butler was reinstated to his position. The butler forgot about Joseph until two years passed when Pharaoh had a dream that troubled him. The butler then remembered Joseph and told Pharaoh about him. God was about to make Joseph's dreams come true (Genesis 40:14).

Heroic Characteristic of Dreams and Interpretation in

Scripture

A Dream is one way God uses to communicate to believers. A godly hero recognizes a dream from heaven and is obedient to it. God can use dreams in many ways: to speak to people (Numbers 12:6-8); to reveal ways to increase wealth (Genesis 31:10); to warn people of danger; (Job 33:14-18; Matthew Ch. 1-2) to reveal secrets in the hearts of men; (Daniel Ch. 2) to show the future;

(Deuteronomy 13:1-5) or to lead you to where you should be (Acts 16:9; 23:11). Dreams are powerful communication tools and the ability to interpret them makes you a godly hero.

To help you understand these four heroic characteristics that made Joseph a hero, there are some questions for you to consider. Take your time and answer these sincerely. Strive to be the best you can be and decide to develop your own heroic qualities. Ask God to help you be an everyday hero.

Questions to consider for your personal growth in becoming an everyday hero like Joseph

1. Has God given you a dream? What do you see yourself doing or being done in your dream?

2. Have you experienced any resistance for what God has put in your heart to do?

3. Have you persisted in doing what God has led you to do even though there is resistance?

4. How do you feel when people are envious or jealous when they see God's goodness in your life?

5. How does having a good attitude even when things don't go your way affect your work? How does a bad attitude affect your work?

6. How easy is it for you to change a bad attitude into a good one?

7. How well do you take care of responsibilities? Are things better when you are there or worse?

8. What temptations do you struggle with? What do you do to overcome them?

9. When things do not go your way or people falsely accuse you of things and forget about you do you maintain an attitude that God would put up with?

10. What gifts, talents & abilities has God given you and how are you using them for His kingdom?

DOUGLAS PYSZKA

Chapter 9

JOSHUA AN EVERYDAY HERO FOR GOD

JOSHUA – Exodus, Deuteronomy and Joshua

Name: JOSHUA a savior; a deliverer [JAHSH oo uh] (the Lord is salvation). The successor to Moses and the man who led the nation of Israel to conquer the land of Canaan and settle the Promised Land.

Hoshea - [hoe SHEE ah] (salvation) - the name of four men in the Old Testament: Another name of Joshua the son of Nun (Num 13:8,16). Hoshea – Salvation; Joshua – The Lord is salvation (Nelson's Bible Dictionary).

Heroic Traits: Super Service, Mighty warrior, Strength in battle, Lasting Loyalty

Mission: Joshua was inaugurated with strength and courage to bring the children of Israel into the land God promised them and God would be with him and distribute Israel's inheritance to them (Deuteronomy 31:23)

Joshua's Heroic Qualities to focus on in being an Everyday Hero:

- He exemplified superior service by serving Moses faithfully until he died.
- He was a mighty warrior who won battles by being strong, gentle and seeking God.
- He was strong & courageous in obeying God and defeating thirty-one kings (Josh. 12:24)
- He was loyal to Moses his leader. He served him and defended him eagerly.

The Challenges Joshua Faced

- He was born in Egypt and grew up as a slave.

- In the land of Canaan, he was a minority.
- He was surrounded by negativity, doubt & unbelief for many years.
- He wandered in the wilderness for forty years based on what others did.

The Magnitude of Joshua's Task

- Joshua was to succeed Moses and complete what he started.
- He was to take people into Canaan and divide the inheritance among the tribes of Israel.
- Joshua was to lead the nation of Israel until they received what was promised to them.
- Joshua had to keep himself from developing a negative & unbelieving attitude for a long time.
- Joshua had to keep his strength and courage to go on and defeat kings who lived in Caanan.

We will study four qualities that distinguished Joshua from others. These qualities made him a hero for God. You also have qualities in you that can transform you into an everyday hero for God.

It is difficult to form an estimate of Joshua's character, because the man is overshadowed by the greatness of the events in which he was placed. This is not meant to dishonor him, but to distinguish him. A lesser man would have been seen and heard more. Joshua did not do things to be seen or heard; he did what the Lord commanded him to do. As a soldier, he was good at following orders.

His life, though recorded with great detail, shows no stain. He was a faithful servant from his youth and he learned how to command others as a man. As a citizen, Joshua was very patriotic; as a warrior, he was fearless and blameless; as a judge, he was calm and impartial. He was well equipped to handle every emergency; and to act decisively and valiantly.

Joshua fulfilled all his duties and no assignment was neglected. He always sought the Lord for guidance and obeyed the Lord's instructions with the simplicity of a child. He also wielded the power he had calmly, without swerving, to accomplish a high, unselfish purpose. He earned by manly vigor a quiet, honored old age and retained his faith and loyalty, exclaiming, in almost his dying breath, "As for me and my house, we will serve the Lord." (Joshua 24:15).

Joshua was one of the twelve men called upon to spy out the land (Numbers 13:16). He was full of the spirit of wisdom after Moses laid his hands on him empowering him to lead Israel (Deuteronomy 34:9).

The Severe Treatment of Canaanites: God created Joshua as a warrior, to fight battles and win. In war, he saw many people die. Joshua acted under God's command to destroy the Canaanites who were excessively wicked (Leviticus 18:20-30). Their acts of sin & lawlessness would contaminate Israel if left alive. (Deuteronomy 7:1-5). They were idolaters that worshiped false gods (El, a monster of wickedness, Baal, god of thunder, Asherah, Anath and Ashtereth – patronesses of sex & war). Be the hero that God has called you to be and rise up and defeat your enemies.

1. Heroic Quality One – Joshua was a Superior Servant

As a hero for God you are a servant of God. A servant does what his master says and carries out his master's instructions diligently. With a good attitude, a servant does what he is asked to do without complaining and with excellence. The Bible tells us Joshua had a heart to serve, "**Joshua did as Moses said to him, and fought with Amalek.**" (Exodus 17:10).

After Israel left Egypt, they encountered their first opponent, the Amalekites, who came and attacked them. Moses told Joshua to choose men and fight with the Amalekites. Moses trusted Joshua with this assignment. As a willing servant, Joshua obeyed Moses, built a team of soldiers and led Israel to defeat the Amalekites (Exodus 17:8-13).

People followed Joshua into battle which showed they trusted his leadership and he led them to victory. As a leader, Joshua: knew his place; did his part; and submitted to the authority of Moses, his leader.

Joshua served Moses many ways. He accompanied Moses as on his way up Mount Sinai; (Exodus 24:13).He assisted Moses in working at the tabernacle in the wilderness. It was here that Joshua learned how to worship God and hear His voice. He watched how Moses communicated with God and would stay there even after Moses left for the day. Joshua went the extra mile by doing more than what was required (Exodus 33:11). Also, he was one of the spies sent to explore Canaan (Numbers 13:2)

Joshua served his whole life and began to serve when he was young. Moses certainly noticed something special about Joshua because he became his mentor (Numbers 11:28-29). Moses changed the name of his protégé from Hoshea to Joshua. The name Hoshea means salvation and the name Joshua means the Lord is salvation. Moses added the Lord to Joshua (Numbers 13:16).

The chain of command: The Lord commanded Moses: who commanded Joshua: *who did* (Joshua 11:15).You can be an everyday hero by learning how to serve others like Joshua did.

The Heroic Characteristic of Service in the Scriptures

The Bible tells you how *you* can be a good servant: A servant should be faithful and wise; he should be reliable, trustworthy and able to rule well; he should be a good manager using all resources in the best and most efficient way; he should take good care of things that do not belong to him and he should be a diligent doer of his master's commands (Matthew 24:45-47).

Joshua was a hero because of the way he served others. He helped Moses whether the circumstance was good or bad, easy or hard, or rough and smooth. Joshua was reliable and dependable at all times. Joshua served because the Lord called him to serve. Perhaps he led well because he served well. Jesus described the greatest person in His kingdom is the servant of all (Matthew 23:11).

A servant is first faithful in little tasks before he is given greater responsibility. Joshua was a hero because he was faithful in the little tasks. He proved his reliability to Moses and developed his leadership through serving others.

The gospel of Luke (19:15-17) tells us about the parable of the minas, a form of currency. A master gave his servants a mina each. Two of the servants took what they were given and multiplied it greatly. One servant did nothing with what he received. He was judged *a wicked servant*, and he lost what he had because it was given to the one who increased his mina ten times. The point of the parable is you must do something with what you have been given and increase it for the Lord otherwise you will lose what you have.

Joshua was one who multiplied what the Lord gave him. He used his *God-given abilities* to serve, to fight battles, take cities and helped Moses with whatever he needed help with. His work increased God's kingdom and expanded His territory.

Do something with what God has given to you. Take your super hero abilities and increase God's kingdom on the earth. Be a faithful and responsible overseer; be a good steward and serve with a good attitude; use the grace that God has given to your advantage and be strong in it (Acts 20:28; 1 Corinthians 4:1-2; Hebrews 3:5; 1 Peter 4:10-11

2. Heroic Quality Two – Joshua was a Mighty Warrior

In his first recorded battle against Amalek at Rephidim, Joshua was assigned the task of choosing men to fight with him against this enemy. Moses was positioned on a hill and Joshua fought on the battlefield. **He led Israel to a victorious battle and defeated their enemy** (Exodus 17). Joshua was a skilled warrior who knew how win by relying on God.

Joshua received a wide range of training to develop his military skill. After defeating Amalek, he was chosen as one of the spies who was sent into Canaan and bring back a report (Numbers 13:8, 16). Joshua developed the skill of a soldier in the Special Forces, by doing reconnaissance. He was able to identify his enemy's strengths & weaknesses, the terrain of the land, and how the land could benefit him if he was led to attack it. He gathered important information, reported to his commander, Moses, and was successful in this endeavor.

Joshua rose up through the ranks of Israel. His faithfulness to God was a key to his success and led him to become commander & leader of Israel when Moses died. Before Moses died, God led him to anoint Joshua as his successor. Israel acknowledged Joshua as their leader (Joshua 1:16-18).

There are two battles that distinguished Joshua as a mighty warrior empowered by God. The first one is Jericho, which was the first city that Israel needed to defeat in the conquest of Canaan. This city was to be offered to God because He had given it to Joshua & Israel (Joshua 6:17-19). Jericho was a city surrounded by a huge wall that was as wide as it was tall. It seemed like an impossible task; but with God all things are possible to them that believe (Mark 9:23).

God gave Joshua a divine plan to beat Jericho. An angel of the Lord appeared to Joshua and he fell down and worshiped the angel and inquired what He had to say. The angel received the worship, which reveals that this was the Lord Himself (Joshua 5:13-15). The plan the Lord gave to Joshua was unconventional; but it proved to be a great success as Joshua implemented it (Joshua 6).

While Joshua was in a covenant with Gibeon, five kings attacked Gibeon because it was a great city. Joshua marched his troops all night long to arrive at Gibeon and help defend it. God spoke to Joshua that He had delivered these five kings into his hands and not a man of them shall stand before him. Having God's Word about a victory, Joshua & his army fought valiantly until their enemy was routed. God even fought with Joshua. The sun was going down and Joshua needed to win because he fought to win every time. He commanded the sun and moon to stand still and they stopped moving which allowed Joshua to utterly defeat his enemies (Joshua Ch. 10). When you are a godly hero, you can do amazing things like Joshua did.

God leads you to fight a good fight of faith. You are always a winner when you fight with faith in God. You can be an everyday hero for God by using your faith to defeat your enemies and overcome your adversary.

The Heroic Characteristics of being a Mighty Warrior in Scripture

As a godly hero, the warfare you are involved in is not a natural fight, but a spiritual fight, that will continue until Jesus returns. God will help you endure and win in this fight because He has provided you with supernatural weapons that are mighty in Him, to pull down strongholds of the mind, where the warfare takes place. The way you fight this spiritual fight is to: Cast down arguments; arrest and capture thoughts that contradict the Bible and commit to fully obeying the Lord (2 Corinthians 10:3-6).

Fighting by faith is accepting Jesus as your Lord, maintaining your relationship with Him for the rest of your life and boldly living for Christ and His cause. The unfailing and proven strategy to win in this spiritual battle is to have faith in God (1 Timothy 6:12).

For this warfare, God provides you with supernatural armor that enables you to overcome the schemes of your enemy, the devil and his army. God's armor makes you strong in His Word and Spirit. The real enemies you face are evil spirits, not people. These spirits are: evil rulers and authorities of the unseen world; mighty powers in this dark world and evil spirits in the heavenly places. God's weapons are much more powerful than any weapon that Satan and his army can utilize (Ephesians 6:10-13). **In God,**

you win!

By accepting Jesus Christ as Lord, you become a soldier in His army. As His soldier, do not let the affairs of life overwhelm you and cause you to lose sight of your divine destiny. God will help you win in every area of your life because He is a winner and wants you to be one also. Make pleasing God your highest priority in life and you will win (2 Timothy 2:4-5).

You increase your strength to fight in this spiritual battle by knowing what God's says about you and believing it wholeheartedly. Your faith in God combined with a clear conscience, makes you victorious. (1 Timothy 1:28-20). Fight well, finish strong and keep the faith and you will be rewarded with a crown of righteousness (2 Timothy 4:7-8).

Joshua was a hero because he was a mighty warrior who fought many battles and won. You can be a mighty hero too because you can fight many spiritual battles and win. God wants to enlist you in His army. Accepting Jesus as your Lord makes you a soldier for Christ. He will lead, guide and direct you how to fight your spiritual battles and win just like he did for Joshua. Be God's warrior and become an everyday hero.

3. Heroic Quality Three – Joshua was Strong & Courageous in Obeying God

God commissioned Joshua to arise, go over the Jordan and take Israel to enter into the land that God has given them. God told Joshua that every place where his foot stepped was his (Joshua 1:1-3).

In order for Joshua to do what God said, God commanded him to be strong and courageous three times (Joshua 1:6-9). As a hero you must be strong & courageous to face challenges. Strength & courage are ingredients to godly faith.

Leaders need strength & courage to make tough decisions, avoid compromising what they believe, and carry out God's will.

When Joshua spied out the land of Canaan, he was in the minority of those who had faith in God. He and Caleb stood against the peer pressure of the majority and conformed to God's will and spoke God's word boldly. Whether anyone stands with you or not, as a hero, determine to stand strong (Numbers 13-14).

When it was time to enter into the land that God promised to give to Israel, Joshua again showed his strength and courage. He took the lead to make sure Israel was ready to enter Canaan by removing the reproach that was on them from wandering in the wilderness. He led them in a purification process to remove the reproach that clung to them. Reproach is the stench and stain that sin and slavery causes and bring people into bondage. The Lord led him to circumcise every male who had been born in the wilderness. Because Joshua was obedient to divine instructions, God removed the reproach that was on them (Joshua 5). With His strength & courage, Joshua lead Israel to be victorious over thirty one kings (Joshua 12:24).

Heroic Characteristics of Strength & Courage in Scripture

When you know God is your source of strength and courage you are fearless. The way you can demonstrate your strength is: by being a man of God; keeping God's commands; walking in His ways and accomplishing His will. His strength will prosper you. God will give you everything you need to succeed including wisdom and understanding. Whatever God instructs you to do will take strength to carry it out.

God will make you strong and courageous which will cause you never to be fearful or dismayed. As you wait on the Lord, actively serving him like a waiter serves a table in a restaurant, He will give you strength. God commands you to be strong and do not fear! If you get into trouble, God will save you. One touch from God will strengthen you, cast out fear from you and give you peace (Daniel 10:18-19).

As a hero, be watchful for opportunities to help others. Stand fast in faith; be brave and strong; let love motivate you. Be strong in God's grace, be strong in the Lord or His Word and be strong in the Power of His Might or have Spiritual power.

(Deuteronomy 31:6; 1 Kings 2:2-3; 1 Chronicles 22:12-13; 1 Chronicles 28:10; 2 Chronicles 32:7-8; Psalm 27:14; Isaiah 35:3-4;1 Corinthians 16:13-14; Ephesians 6:10; 2 Timothy 2:1-2)

4. Heroic Quality Four – Joshua was Loyal

Loyalty is defined as being faithful; trustworthy; devoted; reliable; dependable; steadfast; dedicated and constant. Joshua was a loyal servant of God and Moses. His loyalty lasted through many tests.

Joshua was commissioned by Moses to choose men and fight against Amalek. Joshua was a faithful and devoted follower. Without questioning what Moses said, Joshua went and carried out Moses' command obeying his leader. Every task that Moses gave Joshua was accomplished in a steadfast, dedicated and dependable manner. Joshua was a hero because of his super power of loyalty.

Joshua's loyalty set him apart from others. Joshua accompanied Moses part way up Mount Sinai. His loyalty to Moses gave him access to places others dared not go (Exodus 24:13). Joshua went with Moses to the Tabernacle every day. When Moses left, Joshua remained there experiencing God's presence (Exodus 33:11).

As a loyal hero, Joshua protected Moses from anything that may harm him or negatively affect his leadership. Joshua loved and respected Moses greatly, and defended his honor fiercely (Numbers 11:25-30).

Joshua was loyal to God and His Word. When he returned from surveying the land of Canaan, he gave an accurate report of the land and encouraged the people to go in and take it. He stood by and defended the good report and publically spoke out against the negative report that the others spies gave (Numbers 13:8-17;

14:6-9).

Joshua heeded God's Word and instructions about how to conquer Jericho. He obeyed everything God said and saw the walls of the great city fall flat to make it easy prey for his army (Joshua Ch. 6). Joshua wielded great power without swerving to accomplish a high, unselfish purpose. He encouraged Israel at the end of his to choose to serve God as he chose to do in his family (Joshua 24:15).

God promoted Joshua because of his loyalty. He was chosen to lead Israel after Moses died. God exalted Joshua in the sight of all Israel. God saw how Joshua was loyal to Moses and to Him all his life (Joshua 3:7-8).

Joshua maintained his faith in God, as a minority, for forty years in the midst of a multitude of negative people. He kept his faith in God without swerving. Joshua's loyalty made him a mighty super hero.

Heroic Characteristic of Loyalty in Scripture

Loyalty is serving God with an undivided heart and to be entirely consecrated to Him (Joshua 14:8, 14). When you are loyal to God you heed His commands to love Him; walk in all His ways; hold fast to Him and serve Him with your whole being (Joshua 21:43-45; 22:5).

When you are loyal to God, you will return to Him even when you disobey Him. Loyalty to God means you are disloyal to idols and other gods. You must be exclusive to God and God alone. Get rid of all your idols (1 Samuel 12:20; 7:3; 2 Chronicles 15:15).

When you are loyal to God you keep His covenant and perform all His Words. The Lord God Almighty is the only one worthy of your worship. God is jealous of anything that gets more attention in your life than He does (2 Chronicles 34:31; Deuteronomy 6:13; Matthew 4:10).

To help you better understand the four heroic characteristics that made Joshua a great, godly hero, there are questions for you to consider. Read the questions and sincerely answer them. They will help you to develop your own heroic qualities and help you become an everyday hero.

Questions to consider for your personal growth in becoming an everyday hero like Joshua

1. In what ways do you serve others?

2. As a servant, how well do you handle little tasks like being on time, doing mundane things, focused fully on each task and fully engaged in every assignment?

3. What is your attitude in serving, do you do it for yourself or for God?

4. In facing enemies, how well do you implement God's plan and instructions?

5. Has your skill in warfare increased and do you have more victories than defeats?

6. On a scale from 1 to 10, 1 being the lowest and 10 the highest, how strong & courageous are you?

7. How do you measure your courage? What is the toughest challenge you have faced so far?

8. Are you overcome by fear or do you overcome fear by your faith?

9. What has God assigned you to do? Are you doing what He said?

10. How loyal are you to the leaders that God has placed you with?

11. When you face tough and challenging things, how motivated are you to face them and conquer them?

12. How often does your heart, mouth and soul disagree? What do you do to bring them into agreement?

Chapter 10

MOSES AN EVERYDAY HERO FOR GOD

MOSES – Genesis, Exodus, Leviticus, Numbers and Deuteronomy

Name - MOSES taken out; drawn forth (from Hitchcock's Bible Names Dictionary,

Moses' Heroic Traits: Deliverance, Leadership, Prayerfulness and Meekness

Mission: He was called by God to deliver Israel from Egypt, who was enslaved for over 400 years.

God sent Moses to Pharaoh to bring His people, Israel, out of Egypt (Exodus 3:10).

He made known his ways to Moses, his deeds to the people of Israel (Psalm 103:7).

Nelson's Bible Dictionary says, "Moses was a leader so inspired by God that he was able to build a united nation from a race of oppressed and weary slaves."

Moses Heroic Qualities to focus on in being an Everyday Hero:

- A Mighty Deliverer
- His Strong Leadership
- Powerful Prayerfulness
- His Magnificent Meekness

The Challenges Moses Faced

- He was born in slavery.
- He was marked for death as a baby. Moses was born at a time when the Pharaoh, the ruler of Egypt, had given

orders that no more male Hebrew children should be allowed to live.

- He had to overcome his own insufficiencies and inadequacies to be who God wanted him to be (Exodus 3:11-4:14).
- He had been away from Egypt and his people for forty years.
- He was eighty years of age when he went to Egypt to deliver them.

The Magnitude of Moses' Task

- He had to go back to a nation he left because he was a wanted man for murder.
- He had to lead people out of a hostile country after leading sheep in a desert for forty years.
- God assigned him to deliver a people who were held in bondage for four hundred years.
- He had to face a wicked ruler who was extremely hard-hearted & opposed God.
- He had to set up Israel's system of worship and the laws by which they were to live as a nation.

Moses was the ultimate deliverer, leader, lawgiver, and prophet of Israel. He was the prophet who delivered the Israelites from Egyptian slavery; he was their leader and lawgiver as Israel wandered in the wilderness; he was the son of Amram and Jochebed (Exodus 6:18,20; Numbers 26:58-59), the grandson of Kohath, the great-grandson of Levi, and the brother of Aaron and Miriam.

Moses' Character: To deliver Israel from Egypt, the most powerful nation on the earth at the time, Moses had to be a man of strong character. He stood before Pharaoh many times to demand that God's people be set free. He was fearless, bold and confident in what God had called him to do.

There are four heroic characteristics in Moses that made him a great godly hero. You may have similar qualities in you that will turn you into a godly hero. Seeing Moses' heroic qualities may help you recognize the heroic qualities you possess to become and everyday hero.

1. Heroic Quality One –Moses was a Mighty Deliverer

To deliver means to release; rescue; save; liberate and to free.

God appeared to Moses in a burning bush in the desert. Moses noticed the bush because it was burning but it was not being consumed by the flames. When Moses drew close to the bush, God spoke to him and explained his assignment to him: Moses was to deliver Israel from bondage. He declared Himself to be the God of Abraham, Isaac and Jacob. God saw Israel's oppression, He heard their cry and He knew their sorrows. God knows what happens in the earth at all times and he assigns heroes to solve the problems in the earth (Exodus 3:1-8).

When God brings deliverance, He brings people out of a bad situation and brings them into a much better situation. God delivered Israel from their Egyptian bondage and brought them into a rich fertile land where they were free. God intended to work His will through Moses because He always desires to partner with man. You can be God's partner also and become an everyday hero (Exodus 3:8-10).

Moses accepted God's call even though he was reluctant at first. He appeared before Pharaoh many times and demanded him to release God's people and he performed miracles, signs and wonders which eventually caused Pharaoh to let Israel go. Each display of God's power increased in intensity and severity because Pharaoh's heart became harder and harder. Through Moses, God delivered His people from bondage and oppression.

Heroic Characteristic of Deliverance in Scripture

Joseph was sent to Egypt to deliver Israel from famine and destruction (Genesis 45:7). **All deliverance comes from God, He is your deliverer**. He delivers you from death and He brings you out of trouble and bondage with a very strong hand (Exodus 6:6-8; 12:27; 13:3).

Salvation is deliverance where God comes in and rescues you from an oppressive power. Moses even named one of his son's Eliezer, which means God was my helper and delivered me from Pharaoh's sword (Exodus 14:13; 30; 18:4).

Many good things occur when you are delivered: You are rescued from evil and rejoice; you are released from binding yokes and live in freedom; you stop being a slave; you gain victory over challenges like defeating a bear and a lion bare-handed; you are pulled out of a place marked for destruction before it is destroyed; (Exodus 18:9; 20:2; Leviticus 26:13; Genesis 19:16; 1 Samuel 17:37).

Many heroes experienced God's great deliverance: In Babylon, three young Hebrew men were delivered from a fiery furnace (Daniel 3:27). Daniel was delivered from being consumed by ferocious lions as he slept in their midst (Daniel 6:6; 22). Peter was supernaturally delivered from prison as his chains fell off and doors opened (Acts 5:18).

There are also specific things that God delivers you from: He delivers you from your enemies; (2 Samuel 22:49).God delivered you from hell; (Psalm 86:13).God delivers from the enemies traps; (Psalm 91).God delivers from temptation; (1 Corinthians 10:13; 2 Peter 2;9). Jesus delivers you from death; (2 Corinthians 1:10).God delivers you from every evil work (2 Timothy 4:18).

You can be an everyday hero by using your super powers to deliver someone in danger or facing harm.

2. **Heroic Quality Two – Moses Exercised Great Leadership**

To lead is to manage and control resources, guide others into a specific purpose, be the authority and govern a group.

Moses accepted God's call to lead His people out with a mighty deliverance. He embraced God's call, went into Egypt and ended up delivering one nation from another nation because he was a good leader.

Moses exemplified good leadership: He **followed instructions and proper protocol** in meeting with the elders of Israel to share with them the vision God had given to him (Exodus 4:29-31). As a good leader, **he confronted Pharaoh** who enslaved Israel (Exodus 5:1). **Moses did not quit** until Israel's deliverance took place even though Pharaoh's heart became harder each time Moses faced him.

Israel **followed Moses** and **respected his authority** (Exodus Ch. 12). In fulfilling His purpose, Moses did not lose anything but received everything he demanded of Pharaoh. **He refused to compromise** which made him **a good negotiator**. Moses successfully **led Israel**, with God's help, **through the big obstacles** of the wilderness, the Red Sea and the Egyptian army (Exodus 13; 15-17).

Moses was a good leader because he **delegated authority** and gave others responsibilities; (Exodus Ch. 18).Moses **communicated God's commands** to the people who followed him; (Exodus 19:7).He wrote the laws that governed Israel; (Exodus Ch. 20).

Moses led Israel to **build their corporate headquarters**, their place of worship, the Tabernacle (Exodus Ch. 25-32). He set up a system of worship that enabled Israel to connect with God (Exodus Ch. 25-32). Moses sent leaders to survey the land of Canaan, instructed them to look for specific things, and was able to measure their results (Numbers 13:17-20). As a leader, Moses solved problems like: water & food shortages; people dying from poisonous snake bites; squashing rebellions; corrected people when necessary with God's help and developed winning strategies to defeat his enemies (Exodus Ch. 14).

By increasing and sharpening your leadership skills, you can become a leader like Moses and be an everyday hero.

3. Heroic Quality Three – Moses Prayed Powerfully, it was his Secret Weapon

Every time Moses faced trouble or difficulty, he called on God for help. He and God had a very close relationship. God spoke to Moses as a man would speak to his friend. Moses knew where to find answers to solve all the problems he faced. He received from God power and answers through prayer. His prayerfulness was his super power that he used to help others.

Before Moses faced Pharaoh, he prayed to God to get divine instructions. When things do not work like you think they should, pray (Exodus 5:22-6:1-9). Another type of prayer is intercession. To intercede means to stand in the gap and pray for someone in need because that person may not know how to pray. Moses interceded often for Israel and even Pharaoh when he requested prayer (Exodus 8:8-13; 9:28).

Pharaoh even asked Moses to forgive him. Moses prayed and God forgave (Exodus 10:16-18). You can pray even when you need a basic necessity in life. Israel came to a place where the water was undrinkable. Moses prayed and the Lord answered him and showed him how to make the water drinkable (Exodus 15:25).In another situation, the Israelites came to a dry place that had no water. Moses prayed and God answered him and instructed Moses to strike the rock and water gushed out (Exodus 17:4). Moses' prayers kept many of the Israelites alive (Numbers 14:11-25).

4. Heroic Quality Four – Moses was the Meekest Man

Meekness is not weakness for it receives & releases the strength & power of God. To be meek is to be humble, quiet, gentle and modest. It is to solely rely on God and on nothing else.

Numbers 12:3 reveals to us that Moses was very humble (*meek*), *more than all men who were on the face of the earth*. That is a super hero statement. Moses trusted in God more than himself, or his experiences, in people or in circumstances.

Heroic Characteristic of Meekness in Scripture

As a meek person, you seek the Lord and carry out His commands (Zephaniah 2:3).**You are to receive the Word of God with meekness** (James 1:21). God adds to meekness wisdom and understanding (James 3:13). As a meek person, you pay close attention to how you live and what you teach. You always strive to do what is right (1 Timothy 4:16).

Jesus was meek: Through meekness, He did not open His mouth when He was oppressed and afflicted (Isaiah 53:7). As a meek person, Jesus' gentleness could teach anyone. It doesn't matter what your race is, what your economic status is, what your age is or what you nationality is, you can benefit from meekness. **Meekness is not weakness** but it is a super hero quality (Mathew 11:29).

Meekness is a strength: Paul used the power of meekness to plead his case about what kind of battle the church is in (2 Corinthians 10:1-2). Meekness is strong because **the meek will inherit the earth** and shall delight in an abundance of peace (Psalm 37:11; Matthew 5:5).

The Lord favors meekness: He beautifies the meek and humble with salvation. Only a meek person will trust in the Savior (Psalm 149:4). God is fair to the meek (Isaiah 11:4-5). Those who are meek, lowly, gentle and longsuffering receive tender mercies from the Lord (Colossians 3:12-14). The Lord guides the meek in justice and teaches them His way (Psalm 25:9). It is through meekness that the unity of God's Spirit flourishes (Ephesians 4:2-3).

Meekness is easy to operate: You can put on meekness like you would put on a shirt (1 Timothy 6:11). Meekness is a necessary tool when you must confront and correct those who oppose you. God may grant your opposition repentance after they have witnessed your meekness (2 Timothy 2:24-26). The main tool used to communicate meekness is your mouth. Meekness is speaking gentle words, not harsh words, to all (Titus 3:2).

To help you better understand the four heroic characteristics that made Moses a great, godly hero, there are questions for you to consider. Read the questions and sincerely answer them. They will help you to develop your own heroic qualities and help you become an everyday hero just like Moses.

Questions to consider for your personal growth in becoming an everyday hero like Moses

1. Have you ever been in bondage to anything?

2. Think about things you were delivered from or out of. How did your deliverance take place?

3. Have you been able to help someone else who is in bondage to the same thing you were? What is stopping you from helping someone else?

4. God has made a way for us to be delivered from temptation. What are some ways that you have overcome temptations?

5. Are you a good leader? What are your strengths? What are your weaknesses? How have you developed your leadership skills?

6. Who are some key people in your life that have influenced you to be better and do greater things?

7. Are you producing positive results in your life? Do you feel like you are progressing or retreating?

8. How would you describe your communication with God?

Do you hear His voice and follow Him in all things?

9. Do you pray simply when you need things or is it a daily duty of yours to help you grow spiritually?

10. Who are some people that you have a short fuse with? If you had to be with them for forty days, could you do it?

11. When someone opposes you, how do you correct them?

Chapter 11

MORDECAI AN EVERYDAY HERO FOR GOD

Mordecai - Esther

Name: MORDECAI - contrition; bitter; bruising (from Hitchcock's Bible Names Dictionary)
Heroic Traits: Refusal to bow to evil, Righteousness, Care for family, He honored divine authority
Mission: To raise a queen in a foreign land.

The Bible says in Esther 2:7; 20, "Mordecai had brought up Hadassah, that is, Esther, his uncle's daughter, for she had neither father nor mother. The young woman was lovely and beautiful. When her father and mother died, Mordecai took her as his own daughter. 20 Now Esther had not revealed her family and her people, just as Mordecai had charged her, for Esther obeyed the command of Mordecai as when she was brought up by him."

As you look at Mordecai, ask yourself two questions: The first is, "How well do you respond to pressure?" Mordecai faced pressure to bow to an idol in human form. The second question is, "What kind of things will your life produce?" Mordecai produced a queen that saved her people from being destroyed.

Mordecai Heroic Qualities to focus on in being an Everyday Hero:

- He refused to bow to evil.
- He was righteous.
- He cared for his family.
- He honored divine authority.

The Challenges Mordecai Faced

- He was raised in captivity by a foreign nation. Est 2:6

- He raised his uncle's daughter as his own.
- He had to give Esther up to the king's palace.
- He encountered peer pressure to act against his beliefs.

The Magnitude of Mordecai's Task

- He was raising a daughter to be a queen.
- He did what was right even without recognition. Est 2:19-23
- The person in a position of authority, Haman, hated
  Mordecai & wanted to destroy him.
- He seemed to be in the minority of people who actually
  stand up for what they believe.

There are four qualities about Mordecai that distinguished him from others and made him a hero for God. You may possess similar qualities like Mordecai had or you may have qualities that differ from his. Recognize your distinguishing qualities and become an everyday hero for God too. This is how the Bible describes Mordecai at the end of his life. This is how a hero should be recognized:

> Esther 10:2-3 says, "Now all the acts of his power
> and his might, and the account of the greatness of
> Mordecai, to which the king advanced him, are they
> not written in the book of the chronicles of the kings
> of Media and Persia? 3 For Mordecai the Jew was
> second to King Ahasuerus, and was great among
> the Jews and well received by the multitude of his
> brethren, seeking the good of his people and
> speaking peace to all his countrymen."

Other thoughts about Mordecai

> "Mordecai was truly great, and his greatness gave
> him opportunities of doing the more good. He did
> not disown his people the Jews, and no doubt kept
> to the true religion. He did not seek his own wealth,
> but the welfare of his people. Few have it in their

power to do so much good as Mordecai." Matthew Henry

"If we live by the faith of Christ, we shall be active according to the ability and opportunities he gives us, in promoting his glory and the best interests of men. If our faith be genuine, it will work by love." Matthew Henry

Mordecai was a man who humbled himself. "He that humbles himself shall be exalted" (Matthew 23:12; Luke 14:11; 18:14).

"From sitting contentedly at the king's gate, he was raised to the dignity of highest subject, the powerful ruler of the kingdom. Acting uniformly on the great principles of truth and righteousness, his greatness rested on a firm foundation. His faith was openly avowed, and his influence as a professor of the true religion was of the greatest usefulness for promoting the welfare of the Jewish people, as well as for advancing the glory of God." Jamieson-Fausset-Brown Bible Commentary

"The last we hear of Mordecai, whatever was his after fate, is that he was loyal to his people, and approved himself their benefactor, "seeking the wealth (i.e., wealth—literally, good), and speaking peace to all his seed," all of the stock of Israel." Ellicott's Commentary for English Readers

Esther 10:3. Mordecai the Jew was next unto King Ahasuerus long had he sat contentedly at the king's gate, but now at length he is arrived at the presidency of the king's council. Men of merit may, for a time, seem buried alive; but often, by some means or other, they are discovered and preferred at last.

"His greatness did not make him forget or disown his brethren, nor was he ashamed of his relation to them, though they were strangers and captives,

*dispersed and despised. And they did not envy his
greatness, according to the disposition very
prevalent among mankind in such cases, but
rejoiced in it, and blessed God for it, and
commended and loved him for the right and proper
exercise of his great power." (Benson
Commentary)*

1. Heroic Quality One – Mordecai Refused to Bow to Evil

Do not let evil intimidate you. As a hero, you are in a battle
against evil. Through God, you can confront evil because God in
makes you stronger than it and causes you to win. You must
stand against evil: not honoring it in any way or bowing down to
worship it in any form.

Bowing and prostrating oneself to another could be seen as an
act of worship. Mordecai understood about having no other gods
before the One True God of Israel. Mordecai only committed to
worship God and no one else. Mordecai decided in his heart that
he would not bow to an idol or anything that was evil. He took a
strong stand against evil and often stood alone. The evil that
Mordecai faced came in the form of a man named Haman who
was favored by the king of Persia.

Haman the Agagite was promoted by the king, to a very high
position in the Government, and everyone bowed to him and paid
homage to him. This was a command of the king of Persia.
Bowing to Haman was equivalent to worshiping an idol. Mordecai,
on the other hand, would not bow or pay homage to him because
he worshiped the One True God, not an idol (Esther. 3:2).

Haman was evil. Mordecai stood against Haman so strongly
because he was so evil. Haman was a person who was filled with
wrath and consumed with anger. Because Mordecai, a Jew,
refused to bow to Haman, Haman's hatred went beyond one
person and he hated all Jews and sought to destroy all of them
(Esther 3:5-6).

Haman did not think it was fitting for the Jews to exist because their laws were different than those of other nations. He had a reputation of being an enemy of the Jews. It was his desire to destroy, kill, annihilate and plunder the young, old, children and women of the Jews (Esther 3:8-12).

Haman resented Mordecai and was outraged at his actions of refusing to bow to him (Esther 5:9-11). Haman was a prideful man and celebrated his riches, his children and the positions he was promoted to. Bowing to him would be the same as worshiping a false god. God despises such a vile person as Haman was but He honors those who fear Him (Psalm 15:4).

Mordecai feared God Almighty above all things. His life demonstrated that he sought to please God, not man. He was a hero because he stood up when others bowed down. He not only refused to bow to Haman, but he refused to bow to the evil behind Haman. Be an everyday hero and stand up for God and against evil.

Heroic Characteristic of Refusing to Bow to Evil in Scripture

The Bible commands you not to bow to any idol, any god or worship them or follow their practices (Exodus 20:5; 2; 23:20-26; 2 Chronicles 25:14-15). The ultimate hero, Jesus, was tempted to bow down to Satan and worship him. Jesus swiftly denied Satan's suggestion and boldly declared to him,

"The Word of God says to worship the Lord your God and Him only you shall serve." (Matthew 4:10).

Another example we have is found in the book of Daniel. Three of Daniel's associates, Shadrach, Meshach, and Abed-Nego were commanded by a king to bow down to the statue of gold he made of himself. Every one bowed before the idol of the king, except these three young men. Because they refused to bow, they were thrown in a very hot furnace. **The good news is because they refused to bow to an idol, God brought them through the fire** and they did not even smell like smoke.

Bowing down to evil is a real temptation that heroes face. You will be tempted to pledge your allegiance to things that seek to be glorified by you. You should pledge your allegiance to God and glorify Him alone. You can resist evil like both Mordecai and Jesus did. God protected His heroes that refused to bow to evil and He will protect you too. You are a super hero when you resist evil.

2. Heroic Quality Two – Mordecai was Righteous

What does it mean to be righteous? According to the Greek definition of Romans 1:17, we find it means this: Equity of character or act; Christian justification; innocent, holy, just and right (Strong's New Exhaustive Concordance).

We know that Mordecai was righteous because the Bible records that he was innocent, just, right and displayed high moral character according to God's standard. The degree of righteousness he operated in made him a super hero for God.

Mordecai was righteous in his family. He raised his uncle's daughter for she was an orphan. **It is right to take care of your family** (Esther 2:7). Even though Esther was not his daughter, Mordecai raised her like she was his daughter. That is a right way to do things in God's eyes.

Mordecai was righteous in his actions toward the king of Persia. He overheard a plot to kill king Ahasuerus. He told what he heard to Queen Esther and she told the king in Mordecai's name. He kept the king safe by reporting what he knew. Because he was not afraid to get involved, the king remained alive (Esther 2:19-23)

Mordecai was righteous when he refused to bow to an idol. When the people bowed to Haman, it was the equivalent of bowing to an idol. It was an act of worship. Haman was like a god to the people in Persia. A righteous person does not worship idols but God alone. Mordecai was right not to bow to Haman.

Mordecai was a man who walked in righteousness as a way of life. He whole-heartedly embraced the standards that God laid out in His commandments. Living a righteous life is a powerful way to live. This lifestyle caused Mordecai to overcome his enemy and to inherit all his enemy's assets and property. Mordecai finished strong in a high position of authority in a foreign kingdom. That is the power of righteousness in action.

How Mordecai lived is how we should live in this world. Currently, the world we live in is run by Satan. He is the one who rules the *system* of this world. It takes a strong man to live in this world according to a different standard and not lose or compromise his way. You can live righteously in an evil world. You can truly be above and not beneath. Living a righteous life is the life of an everyday hero.

The Heroic Characteristic of Righteousness in Scripture

The kings of Judah represented a righteous line of kings in the Bible. Hezekiah and Asa were two kings of Judah. **They both did what was right, good and true in God's sight.** Each of them was rewarded by God for their stance for righteousness. God loves righteousness and justice; they are the foundation upon which His throne rests (2 Chronicles 14:2; 31:20; Psalm 33:5; 89:14).

The super power of righteousness causes you to seek and follow after the Lord. The Lord is the epitome of righteousness because He is righteous in all His ways. Righteousness is the nature of God and being born of Him makes you righteous (Isaiah 51:1-2; Psalm 145:17; 119:137; 1 John 2:29).

Zachariah and Elizabeth served the Lord and were advanced in age. Zechariah was a priest and Elizabeth was a descendant of Aaron, God's first high priest. **They were both righteous before God, blameless and followed His commands.** They did not have children and now they were too old. God rewarded their righteousness by giving them a son which they named John. Righteousness is powerful (Luke 1:5-6).

3. **Heroic Quality Three – Mordecai Raised his Family to be Godly**

How a person leads, interacts and communicates to their family matters to God. God knew how Abraham interacted with his family; and how he commanded them in the way of the Lord to live righteously and justly (Genesis 18:19).

Mordecai took on the responsibility of raising his uncle's daughter, Esther. Her parents died and Mordecai raised her as his own daughter. He did not know at the time, but what he was to instill in his daughter was everything she needed to become a queen.

Esther kept Mordecai's instruction by not revealing her true identity as a Jew, which protected her. She obviously respected Mordecai and followed his instructions. Following godly wisdom preserves life. Mordecai also respected Esther as the Queen of Persia (Esther 2:20). Mordecai and Esther demonstrated how a family should be united: They respect one another; love each other; help each other and care for each other (Esther 4:17).

Mordecai was very involved in Esther's life. When she was chosen to be a candidate for queen, Mordecai paced in front of the women's quarters daily to learn of Esther's welfare and what was happening to her (Esther 2:11). You should be very involved in your family and there should be fellowship, dialogue and interaction with each member of the family. Be an everyday hero to your family.

Heroic Characteristics of Leading a Family Well in Scripture

Here are truths to help you lead your family well and be a hero to them: Keep yourself in order and spiritually fit by practicing what you preach (Deuteronomy 4:9). Put God's word in your heart and teach others with your actions and words. Have conversations about God's word in your home (Deuteronomy 6:6-9).

Make it a priority to know God and practice what He said in your home and lead by example. Your children need to **see you follow God, before they hear what you have to say about**

following God. If your family is not serving the Lord than whom are they serving? Decide that your house will follow the Lord unashamedly (Deuteronomy 11:19-21; 32:46; Joshua 24:15).

Develop your own relationship with the Lord and be loyal to Him. Following God's commands are a lamp and a light to you. Through God's Word and His Spirit you are equipped with everything you need to lead your family in the right way. It is your job to train your children in *the way they should go* and the way they should go is the way of Jesus who is the Way. You will advance in God's kingdom by ruling your own house well. Lead your family in righteousness (1 Chronicles 28:9; Proverbs 6:20-23; 22:6; 1 Timothy 3:3-4).

The thought of being the spiritual leader of your home may be gut-wrenching but it is what you are called to do. Rising up to meet this challenge will transform you into a powerful super hero for God and super heroes overcome any challenge.

4. Heroic Quality Four – Mordecai Honored Divine Authority

The Bible recorded Mordecai, as a man who feared God. He had the utmost respect and reverence for God and His divine authority. When a person fears God, they honor, reverence and respect Him, His places and His people. Those who fear God live out what they believe confidently, without being afraid. Honoring divine authority is being faithful in little things, being diligent and speaking up when necessary. It is putting into practice the principles God gives us in His Word.

Mordecai honored the king's authority by stopping a plot to kill him (Esther 2:19-23). When you honor authority, God will honor you. Mordecai was eventually honored because honored authority.

As mentioned, **a person who honors authority does not bow to idols**. Mordecai refused to bow to Haman because his heart and love was to worship God exclusively. God is the ultimate authority. He should be honored and His commands upheld above all. Even when people pressured him daily, Mordecai would not compromise what he believed to be right, true and just. He put himself at risk because he was disobeying a command of the king. He was not fearful (Esther 3:2-5).

Mordecai also put his trust in God and he did not lean unto his own understanding. When he told Esther what Haman was going to do with the Jews, he also told her that deliverance would arise from another place to save the Jews if she refused to take action. He placed his confidence in God alone (Esther 4:14)

The Characteristics of Honoring Divine Authority in Scripture

In Numbers 20:12, the Israelites faced another water shortage. This time God instructed Moses to speak to the rock before the elders of Israel. Out of anger, Moses struck the rock instead of speaking to it. Water came out but because Moses and Aaron did not honor God in obeying Him, they were disqualified from entering into the land God promised to give to Israel. Dishonoring God is costly (Numbers 20:12).

Eli was a priest of God. God called the sons in Eli's family to be priests forever but they despised the Lord. His two sons were wicked and vile in God's sight and Eli did not discipline his children. Therefore, no man was left alive in Eli's heritage. They all died, not fulfilling what God called them to do (1 Samuel 2:22-36).

Thinking, speaking or acting contrary to God's word breeds confusion and shame and dishonors the Lord. **You are to glorify God in all you do**. Make it your goal to live a life that honors God and makes knowing Him and doing His will the most important priority in your life. God is a personal God who comes to where you are so He can bring you where He is. The Lord is the King: He is eternal; He is immortal; He is invisible; He is all knowing and He alone should be honored and glorified (Psalm 35:26-28; Isaiah 25:1; 1 Timothy 1:17).

The four heroic qualities that Mordecai displayed in his life made him a super hero for God. You may have similar super qualities like Mordecai had or yours may differ from his. Recognize and develop your super hero characteristics and be an everyday hero.

To help you better understand how Mordecai was a godly hero, consider the following questions and answer them sincerely and improve your skill in being an everyday hero also.

Questions to consider for your personal growth in becoming an everyday hero like Mordecai

1. How well do you perform under pressure?

2. On the current path you are on, what do you think your life will produce? How will others benefit from your life?

3. If you were the only one doing the right thing, would you continue to do what is right?

4. What is your greatest temptation? How do you overcome it?

5. What kind of relationship do you have with your family? Is there mutual respect, communication and love in your family?

6. Do you fear God? How does fearing God influence your behavior privately and publicly?

7. If you uncovered a plot to harm this country's leader, what would you do about it?

8. Are there any idols in your life? If God were to identify something or someone in your life as an idol, what would you do about it?

9. When you do not understand why something is happening or why it is not working out like you want it to, does your speech turn negative or stay positive?

10. Do you solve more problems than you create or do you create more problems than you solve?

Chapter 12

ELISHA AN EVERYDAY HERO FOR GOD

Elisha – 1 & 2 Kings

Name: Elisha - Salvation of God   (from Hitchcock's Bible Names Dictionary)
Heroic Traits: A double anointing, Spirit of Victory, Great Spiritual Vision Commanding Authority.
Mission: Elisha was called to be a prophet of God and to be Elijah's successor.

Elisha's Heroic Qualities that Made Him an Everyday Hero:

- Elisha was called to be a prophet of God and he dedicated his life to fulfill that call.
- Elisha lived in a spirit of victory over his enemies, over greed and over evil.
- Elisha was a man of great spiritual vision and he knew what God gave him.
- Elisha had strong commanding authority and his words released the miraculous.

Challenges Elisha Faced:

- He completely changed careers. Before Elisha was a prophet, he was a farmer. He was plowing with twelve yoke of oxen when God's call came to him.
- He left all he knew and was familiar with: his family, his farming; his home and his friends.
- He served Elijah who was depressed, intimidated and fearful after running from Jezebel's threats.

- Although he was called to be a prophet, he started out serving, not prophesying.

The Magnitude of His Task:

- Elisha needed to make a quick decision and take swift action to fulfill his call. God must have been preparing him before hand and perhaps he had an inkling a prophet would cross his path.
- He swiftly changed direction in his life from ploughing to prophesying and proclaiming God's word.
- He ventured into the unknown willingly. He acted like Abraham did when he left into the unknown.
- He served Elijah wholeheartedly, a rough and solitary individual, who adopted Elisha as his son.

1. Heroic Quality One – Elisha had a Double Portion Anointing

Elijah, a prophet of God, was commanded by God to anoint Elisha as prophet in his place. God revealed to him who would take his place. Elijah found Elisha plowing with oxen. Elijah threw his mantle or coat on Elisha signifying that he was called to be a prophet and he would be like a son of Elijah. Elisha's heart was touched by the Holy Spirit, and he was ready to leave all to serve Elijah (1 Kings 19:19-21).

Elisha ran after Elijah for two reasons: he understood the meaning of the mantle being placed on him; he made up his mind at once to pursue God's call & training wholeheartedly. Elijah did not demand Elisha's service, but allowed him to freely choose to follow him and learn from him.

Matthew Henry, a Bible Commentator and a preacher of the 18th century said, "Elijah found Elisha by divine direction, not in the schools of the prophets, but in the field; not reading, or praying, or sacrificing, but ploughing. Idleness is no man's honor, nor is husbandry any man's disgrace. An honest calling in the world does not put us out of the way of our heavenly calling, any more than it did Elisha." (Matthew Henry).

After serving Elijah for about eight years, **Elisha qualified to inherit a portion that a first born son would receive from his father**. Elijah accepted and treated Elisha like his own son; therefore, Elisha qualified to receive a double portion of the anointing. He faithfully ministered to Elijah.

At the end of their ministry together Elijah asked Elisha, "*Ask! What may I do for you, before I am taken away from you*?" Elisha said, "*Please let a double portion of your spirit be upon me.*" So he said, "You have asked a hard thing. **Nevertheless, if you see me when I am taken from you, it shall be so for you; but if not, it shall not be so**." (2 Kings 2:9-11).

This request demonstrated to God & Elijah that Elisha greatly valued and respected spiritual things or the things of God. **Elisha wanted to be equipped to serve God more than anything else**. Elijah told his protégé that he asked for a hard thing; but his request would be granted if Elisha saw his mentor be taken up. Elisha did not leave Elijah's side and saw him when he was taken up and received a double portion of the anointing that was on Elijah's life.

Elisha picked up Elijah's mantle as it fell from the sky and the first thing he did was to divide the Jordan River; to crossover to the other side. The sons of the prophets from Jericho recognized that the Spirit of Elijah rested on Elisha (2 Kings 2:15). With a double portion of Elijah's anointing, Elisha performed twice as many miracles as Elijah did and lead him to live a triumphant life interacting with his fellow men.

Elisha served as a prophet in Israel for about sixty years (B.C. 892-832). There is no record that he ever: complained of his circumstances; fled from his enemies; lost his courage. He was so powerfully anointed, that after he died his bones even brought a dead soldier to life when he touched them as he fell in his grave (2 Kings 13:21). As a godly hero, he had power in his bones.

Elisha's double anointing was witnessed by the miracles he performed. He performed the highest number of miracles in the Old Testament – second only to Moses. His miracles answered a wide variety of needs in every level of society. He carried out signs and wonders for high government officials, peasants and the disadvantaged. Elisha's double anointing made him an everyday hero for God. Know that God has anointed you also and with His anointing you can become an everyday hero.

The Heroic Characteristics of a Double Portion in Scripture

God is a God of increase and multiplication. He always does more than you expect. He gives you double honor with everlasting joy for shame you may endure (Isaiah 61:7). Job was a man in the Bible who lost his wealth, his children and his health in one day. His entire body broke out in boils and sores that were very painful. His wife wanted him to curse God and die (Job 1:13-19).

God did not leave Job this way. **God blessed Job at the end of his life more than the beginning**: He doubled his livestock; gave him ten more children; his three daughters were the most beautiful women in the land; Job's years were extended to one hundred and forty; he saw his grandchildren for four generations. God knows how to turn things around (Job 42:12-17).

God teaches believers to give double honor to pastors who rule well and labor in the Word of God (1 Timothy 5:17).

Jesus promised those who followed him wholeheartedly that they would do what He did and they would do greater things. The greater things we do are greater in scope; greater in number and in more places. The Lord also promised King Cyrus that he would subdue nations, disarm kings and have double doors opened for him to give him treasure and riches (Isaiah 45:1-3).

Jesus is a multiplier and anything you give to Him, including your life, He will multiply it greatly. God can give you double of whatever you need to help you become an everyday hero for God.

2. Heroic Quality Two – Elisha Lived in a Spirit of Victory Continually

In 2 Kings 6, the Bible shows us the king of Syria was making war with Israel. The King of Syria would meet with his advisory council to make plans to attack Israel. **God would reveal to Elisha the secret plans that Syria made** and Elisha warned the King of Israel to avoid the place that the Syrians were going to attack and Israel would be delivered from their enemies.

The Syrians are just like the devil's cohorts. The devil makes plans to steal, kill and destroy Christians, but God reveals those plans to those who truly believe in and listen to Him so they can avoid being stolen from, killed or destroyed.

God has made it possible for you to have victory over any enemy. Elisha lived a victorious life and overcame every challenge he faced because he lived close to the Lord and communicated with Him regularly. The King of Syria was told that Elisha was the one who revealed the plans of Syria to Israel. So he sent his army to capture Elisha.

Syria discovered that it was Elisha who warned Israel of their impending ambushes. They wanted to capture Elisha and surrounded the city where he resided. Elisha's servant realized they may be captured. He was fearful and wondered what Elisha would do. When he told Elisha what was about to happen, Elisha showed no fear because he lived in victory. He was fully persuaded that God was his protector, deliverer and shield. He could see God's angelic host around him (2 Kings 6:15-17).

Elisha prayed for his servant's eyes to be opened and his servant saw what Elisha saw, fiery horses and chariots around

Elisha. A godly hero has a mighty army encamped around him. The Lord struck the Syrian army with blindness at Elisha's command, and they all were blind. That is powerful! God will show you how to respond to those who come against you.

Living in a spirit of victory means two people can defeat and capture an army of many that comes against you, without raising a sword or having a shield. Elisha used the Word of God as his spiritual weapon and defeated his enemy. He captured all the Syrians that came against him with a word, and led the blind Syrian army straight to the King of Israel. When they arrived, he commanded their eyes to be opened. Elisha did not let the Syrians die but fed them then released them. His victory over the Syrians was so decisive that they did not come against Israel again (2 Kings 6:23). When you know you are the Lord's, you are a spiritual powerhouse; God's angels are around you and He makes you unstoppable so you can become an everyday hero.

The Heroic Characteristics of Victory in the Scriptures

If Jesus is your King: He commands victories to occur for you; He pushes down your enemies and tramples those who rise against you (Psalm 44:4-8). The Lord enables you to tread upon the lion and the cobra without being harmed and even if Satan comes against you with all his power, he cannot hurt you! (Psalm 91:13; Luke 10:19).

You are more than a conqueror in Christ Jesus. He will always lead you to triumph. He provides you with powerful weapons that demolish strongholds. If you are born of God, you can overcome the world through your faith. Within every child of God resides the Greater One and He is greater than anyone in the world. Be thankful to God who gives you the victory through Jesus Christ! (Romans 8:37; 2 Corinthians 2:14; 10:4; 1 John 4:4; 5:4; 1 Corinthians 15:57).

3. **Heroic Quality Three – Elisha had Great Spiritual Vision**

Elisha had great spiritual insight. He recognized the importance of leaving the life of agriculture and entering into a life of the prophetic (1 Kings 19:20-21). He saw the potential in serving a seasoned prophet like Elijah. He saw God's angels around him wherever he went.

Elisha's greatest endowment, the anointing of God, came to him because **he saw** his mentor leave the earth. **He needed to see Elijah being taken up** to receive the anointing, so that when **he saw the prophet's mantle fall**, he could literally pick it up and begin to use it. Elisha stayed focus on the goal and resisted many opportunities that would cause him to miss his opportunity (2 Kings 2:10-12). He did not let Elijah out of his sight. His vision was his super power that made him a godly hero.

Elisha had the ability to recognize important things from a great distance away. He saw the Shunammite woman afar off. She was in distress and needed a miracle. Her miracle boy was dead but her faith was working and God used Elisha to bring her son back to life (2 Kings 4:25).

Elisha had insight into his spiritual protection detail that was assigned to him, God's fiery angels; and he knew that he could call on them anytime he needed to. They were there to help him and he could see them (2 Kings 6:16-17).

Elisha's spiritual insight and vision made him a hero for God and you can be an everyday hero for God too, as the Lord will open your eyes to see great things.

The Heroic Characteristics of Spiritual Vision in the Scriptures

God enables His close followers to know His mysteries, have hidden truth revealed to them and understand spiritual realities that are not seen through natural means (Matthew 13:11-17). As a disciple of Jesus, you can look to Him for faith begins and ends with Him (Hebrews 12:1).

Stephen, a disciple of Jesus, was full of faith and power and performed great signs and wonders among the people. He experienced a vision where the heavens opened up and he saw Jesus giving him a standing ovation. He was so inspired that he forgave the people who were stoning him to death (Acts 7:55).

Jesus told a disciple, Nathaniel, that he would see greater things. He was enabled to see heaven opened and angels going up and down on Jesus. Faith in the Lord Jesus increases vision (John 1:50-51). Imagine what you could see with Jesus' help that you are not seeing now. Let Jesus increase your vision.

Jesus will open your understanding to comprehend what He is saying in the Scriptures (Luke 24:45). God will show secret truths that are hidden in His kingdom. He will reveal to you His success principles that will promote you and bless you. The Lord will even show you where your enemy has placed traps and help you avoid getting caught in them. There are many things to see beyond the natural realm. God will do amazing things for you as you allow Him to open your eyes to see into the unseen and become an everyday hero.

4. Heroic Quality Four – Elisha had Commanding Authority

The authority of heaven is revealed through righteous hearts and mouths. Elisha was a prophet of God and when he spoke things happened. When you are right with God and walking with God, you will speak with authority. Many people recognized that Jesus and His apostles spoke with authority.

When you possess and recognize your authority, your words will inspire others to take action.

Having authority to command is very important in being an everyday hero. God used His commanding authority to create this world and everything in it. When Elisha spoke, things changed and people followed his commands. His commanding authority made him a hero for God. When you get into God's commands and they get into you, you will be a commander in God's kingdom and a mighty hero for Him.

As mentioned before, Elisha saw Elijah when he was taken up into heaven. He didn't just gaze into the sky wondering what was happening, but he made a demand upon the anointing of God and cried out, "My Father, my Father." Elisha said these words to remind God of the relationship that he had with Elijah. Elisha made this decree to possess the double portion of Elijah's spirit that he was promised (2 Kings 2:12).

As Elijah's mantle fell from the sky, Elisha tore his clothes and took up Elijah's mantle and made it his. He was now ready to step into the position he was called to. He took the mantle and struck the waters of the Jordan and said, "Where is the Lord God of Elijah?" When he did this, the waters of the Jordan were divided and Elisha crossed over on dry ground. His commanding authority gave him the double portion he requested and qualified to receive. He now could function as the prophet God made him to be.

In 2 Kings 3, Israel and Judah joined forces to fight the Moabites who rebelled against Israel. As the armies went to battle, they did not have any water for the army or for their animals. Jehoshaphat, King of Judah, called for a prophet and he recognized that Elisha had the Word of the Lord.

Elisha asked for a musician; as he played, the hand of the Lord came on him. Elisha spoke the Word of the Lord with authority. He told the army to make the valley full of ditches; and they would not see the wind nor see rain; yet the valley will be filled with water. Elisha described this as a simple matter in the sight of the Lord. He also declared that God would give the Moabites into your hands. The words of Elisha came to pass as the valley was filled with water (2 Kings 3:20).

A prophet of God speaks God's words and causes miracles to occur. God gave Elisha divine authority to speak to circumstances and they changed.

He spoke to a widow woman who was in debt and gave her a divine strategy to pay her debt off and live. Elisha declared that a woman, who had no children, would have a son and it came to pass just as he had declared. He commanded a Syrian general, Naaman to dip in the Jordan seven times to be healed of leprosy. The general's skin was like the skin of a baby (2 Kings 4:1-7; 16-17; 6:8).

Elisha's commanding authority made him a hero for God. You can command God's commands and they will work for you also so you can be an everyday hero for God.

The Heroic Quality of Commanding Authority in the Scriptures

Jesus met a Roman centurion who really understood how authority operated. His servant was sick so he came to Jesus. Jesus was willing to go to his house and heal his servant, but the centurion was not comfortable with that. He told Jesus just to give the command and his servant would be healed. Jesus marveled at how much faith this centurion had and described his faith as the greatest faith in Israel (Matthew 8:8).

Jesus has authority over evil spirits. A man was mute because he was demon-possessed. Jesus cast the demon out and the man spoke. All the witnesses said *nothing like this* was ever seen in Israel. Jesus showed His authority by commanding evil spirits, including unclean spirits, to leave people (Matt 9:32-34; Mark 1:27).

Jesus spoke to a paralytic man and declared that his sins are forgiven and commanded him to rise up and walk and he got up. Jesus spoke to the wind and to the waves that were raging in a storm and they calmed down instantly. Every believer that has made Jesus their Lord has the same authority to do what Jesus did. He authorized them and commissioned them to go and preach and teach on His behalf (Mark 2:5-12; 4:41; Matthew 218:18-20).

If you are a Christian who is filled with God's Spirit, then you have commanding power in you along with other God-given qualities. As they are discovered and developed; you can be an everyday hero for God.

To help you understand the characteristics that made Elisha a godly hero, consider the following questions. Take time to answer them sincerely to develop your super powers.

Questions to consider for your personal growth in becoming an everyday hero like Elisha

1. What is your attitude toward spiritual things or things of God? Which do you invest more of yourself in, natural endeavors or spiritual endeavors?

2. How quickly do you respond to God when He asks you to do something you have never done?

3. Which is more important to you; money, fame, notoriety, a high position, your family or the anointing of God? Why?

4. Are you more confident in God and his protection and care for you than you are fearing what might happen to you when danger or difficulty arises in your life?

5. Do you walk and live in a spirit of victory or do you find yourself being defeated by things that come against you?

6. Have you considered the weight of the words you speak? Would others describe you as having commanding authority?

7. Are your words positive or negative? Do your words inspire or tear down? When you speak do things happen?

8. Would you be faithful and loyal enough to God to receive a double portion of your mentor's spirit?

9. Who are your mentors?

DOUGLAS PYSZKA

Chapter 13

DANIEL AND EVERYDAY HERO FOR GOD

Daniel – Book of Daniel

Name: Daniel - Judgment of God; God my judge (from Hitchcock's Bible Names Dictionary)
Heroic Traits: Self-control, Courage, Prayerfulness, Integrity
Mission: He was to be an anointed statesman and serve in a foreign king's court.

Daniel's Heroic Qualities that Made Him an Everyday Hero:

- Daniel exercised self-control as he purposed not to defile himself by eating certain foods.
- Daniel was courageous and spoke up when necessary and confronted people.
- Daniel was a disciplined person of prayer. Nothing could stop him from praying.
- Daniel had very high integrity in his workplace and in his relationships.

Challenges Daniel faced:

- He was taken from his home and sent to a foreign country as a captive.
- He was examined and scrutinized as he underwent training to serve in the king's court.
- Because he was promoted to prominent positions, his peers were envious & jealous of him.
- He had to work with many ungodly and worldly leaders.

The magnitude of his task:

- His faith in God set him apart from many. He lived differently because of his faith.
- Governments don't tend to let foreigners hold high positions especially captives.
- Daniel was a captive. His country was invaded and defeated and he was sent away.
- People who practice holiness, live purely and have integrity are considered strange to the world.

1. Heroic Quality one – Daniel Displayed Self-Control

Daniel was a man who lived out his commitment to God in everyday life. As an exile in a foreign land, Daniel experienced God's favor and he rose to a very high position in the government and served four kings. He held true to his values and would not compromise his convictions. He trusted in God with his whole heart. Going to God in prayer was his first response to every challenge he faced.

Daniel was chosen to be trained to serve in the king's court in Babylon. For three years, he learned the ways of Babylon and studied their culture. Part of his training consisted of eating the king's delicacies and drinking his wine that was given to him (Daniel Ch. 1).

Daniel purposed in his heart not to defile himself with these things. He was not going to eat food that was probably sacrificed to idols because he decided in his heart that he was going to honor God in all he did. Daniel asked the person overseeing him if he could eat only vegetables, drink water and he allowed his supervisor to watch him closely. The results were amazing. Daniel and his three associates looked better than all others who were being trained. God honored his self-control and gave him divine favor.

Daniel purposed in his heart not to be defiled. There was something about the king's food that Daniel felt would defile him if he ate it. He chose not to partake of the royal delicacies, going against logic or reason, but he chose to deny himself and stay pure. His decision showed determination, resolve and purpose. King Nebuchadnezzar looked for people who possessed these qualities. God looks for a strong heart like Daniel's to make decisions and see them through to the end.

Daniel was a person who was good looking, gifted in wisdom, educated, quick to understand, able to serve in the palace and one who could learn the Chaldean language and literature. God helped Daniel do this. Daniel's self-control caused him to be a godly hero.

The Heroic Characteristic of Self-Control in the Bible

Self-control is a by-product of the work of God's Spirit in a believer's heart. As a hero, if you compete for a prize, you must be temperate or self-controlled in all things. Winning requires you to be disciplined. Controlling yourself is a great super power. If you do not control yourself, than who is controlling you? A temptation that everyone faces is to over indulge. You prevent that from happening by exercising self-control and become an everyday hero (Galatians 5:22; 1 Corinthians 9:25-27; Titus 1:6-9)

2. Heroic Quality Two – Daniel was Courageous

Daniel was not afraid to speak up when a situation needed a voice. Daniel spoke to the chief eunuch about not eating the king's food. Daniel had to convince him to allow him to do something different than everybody else (Daniel 1:8). God honored Daniel's integrity and courage by giving him favor with the chief (Daniel 1:9).

Daniel also had to trust God completely because he suggested to the chief that he and his friends be tested to see a noticeable difference. **Courageous people trust God, take Him at His Word and live by faith**. Their faith in God never lets them down.

God honored Daniel by giving him knowledge and skill in all

literature and wisdom; and he had understanding in all visions and dreams (Daniel 1:17). Daniel and his friends stood out above the rest. They were ten times better than all the magicians & astrologers in the realm. The king chose them to serve before him. It was his courage that made the difference.

Daniel talked to the captain of the guard and to the king about having more time to be able to interpret the king's dream (Daniel 2:16). After interpreting the king's dream, Daniel **showed courage in witnessing for God and giving Him all glory**. The enemy tries to steal or stop your courage; but do not yield to him (Daniel 2:27-28). You do what is right in God's sight even if it is not popular. In life, you will face pressure like Daniel did. Maybe you will be pressured to not do anything or say anything but as a hero, do something and say something.

Daniel also acted courageously when he encouraged King Belshazzar to do what is right and change his ways (Daniel 3:27). You could let fear paralyze you- which is what the devil wants; or you could stir up courage in your heart and act and speak when an opportunity is open. Be a courageous everyday hero!

Heroic Characteristics of Courage in Scripture

God commands you to be strong and courageous. As you wait on the Lord, courage will come to you. God's strength produces godly courage which stands up strong for what is right. It takes great courage to refuse to participate in evil, no matter how much pressure is applied to you to get you to compromise what you believe is true. Courage speaks up when others are silent and courage does what God says above what man says (Joshua 1:6-9; Psalm 27:14; 31:24; 1 Chronicles 22:13; Daniel 3:16-18; Acts 5:29-33).

3. Heroic Quality Three – Daniel was Prayerful

Daniel knew how to have a conversation with God. He was

well skilled in the art of prayer. He knew how to pray and have God respond in miraculous ways. When his life and his friend's lives were threatened, he went to pray and seek God's mercies (Daniel 2:17).

The king had issued a decree that all the wise men in Babylon should be killed. Some died. Daniel gathered with his friends and they sought God to reveal the secret of the king's dream. The king told no one what he dreamed but he wanted an interpretation of it without saying anything about it. What seemed like an impossible task became possible because Daniel & his friends prayed (Daniel 2:19).

Daniel prayed frequently and habitually. When Daniel's associates wanted to get rid of him, they could only accuse him of praying to someone other than the king. They deceived the king into signing a law that prevented anyone from praying to anyone else except the king for thirty days. Upon reading the law, Daniel went home, opened his windows and doors and prayed three times a day on his knees (Daniel Ch. 6).

Prayer was the basis of Daniel's life. It was the bedrock upon which his life was founded. He lived a lifestyle of communicating with God in prayer. Nothing could stop Daniel from praying. His prayerfulness made him a hero for God.

Heroic Characteristic of Prayer in Scripture

Prayer is such an important heroic characteristic that it should be done many times a day. Prayer is communicating with God and setting your face towards Him. Wrap every prayer to God with praise to Him. As you abide in the Lord and His Words abide in you, your prayers are powerful and effective. Ask God for what you need, want and desire. Prayer seeks an audience with the Lord and knocks on His door (Psalm 55:17; Daniel 9:3-5; John 15:1-8; Matthew 7:7-12).

Praying to God will bring His peace that passes understanding to you and eliminates anxiety from your life. Just like there are different rules for different sports, there are different types of prayer that cover different situations. As a hero, you need to be able to pray effectively. It is a powerful weapon in fighting evil (Philippians 4:6-8; Ephesians 6:18).

4. Heroic Quality Four – Daniel had High Integrity.

Integrity is honesty, honor and uprightness. Daniel was a politician who lived above reproach by doing what was right in God's sight and according to God's standard. We see early on how Daniel strives to please God and not man by not wanting to defile himself with the king's food (Daniel Ch. 1).

After interpreting the king's dream, Daniel was promoted to a high position. He became the ruler of the whole province of Babylon and chief administrator over all the wise men. As a man of integrity, Daniel didn't forsake his friends who prayed with him. In Daniel 2:49, Daniel also gets his friends promoted. This was not just a political payback; but Daniel was genuine and sincere in his relationships.

In Daniel 4:8-9, the king recognized Daniel as one who has the Spirit of the Holy God. The king knew that no secret troubled Daniel and that Daniel could interpret what the king saw. Daniel's life demonstrated that even though he held high positions of authority, he was not corrupted, he did not compromise and he caused righteousness to be exalted.

Daniel was not arrogant when he interpreted dreams. He respected the positions of authority that he spoke to. He advised the king to stop sinning, live righteously and show mercy to the poor. He encouraged him and suggested the king that his prosperity may be lengthened. His integrity and courage worked together as he spoke what was right to the king and God (Daniel 4:27).

It is recorded in Daniel 5:11-13 that Daniel was described as having an excellent spirit, which is integrity (Daniel 6:3). He had great skill in knowledge, understanding, interpreting dreams, solving riddles and explaining enigmas; but he never was prideful about his gifts and abilities. He always gave glory to God. He never demanded anything for his gifts & abilities; and God abundantly blessed him.

The Bible describes n Daniel 6:4: Daniel was faithful; he did not commit errors or show faults. His integrity was impeccable. Even the king spoke of Daniel as one who served God continually (Daniel 6:16). Daniel declared to the king that God sent His angel to deliver him from the lions because he was found innocent before Him; and that he had done no wrong. In verse 23, Daniel believed in his God and he lived by his faith (Daniel 6:22).

An angel appeared before Daniel and told him that he was greatly beloved. Now, when God says you are greatly beloved, you are doing something right. God is in favor of righteousness and holiness which are two key components of integrity. Daniel's integrity made him a hero for God and you can be a man of impeccable integrity to be an everyday hero too (Daniel 9:23).

Heroic Characteristic of Integrity in Scripture

Jesus values a pure heart and said, "Blessed are the pure in heart, they shall see God." (Matthew 5:8)

Being a person of integrity means you have a narrow focus and concentrate on doing what is right in God's sight; it is striving to please God and not man; it is doing things out of a pure heart with pure motives; it is walking uprightly, doing what God says and letting God's Word be the foundation of your life. The Lord has great joy to know His children walk in truth (Matthew 6:22-23; 6:1-4; 1 Kings 9:4-7; Psalm 18:21-24; Proverbs 11:3; 3 John 1:3-4).

To help you better understand the qualities that Daniel possessed to make him a godly hero, consider the following questions and take time to answer them sincerely. Make any adjustments that you need to make and correct what you need to correct and continue to develop in becoming an everyday hero!

Questions to consider for your personal growth in becoming

an everyday hero like Daniel

10. Are you a self-controlled person or are you out of control?

11. In what ways do you display self-discipline?

12. How often do you speak up to validate your faith or avoid compromising what you believe to others?

13. Do you feel comfortable speaking to people in a high position of authority; or are you intimidated by their position?

14. How would you describe your prayer life? Do you see positive results from your prayers?

15. When something good happens in your life, to whom do you direct the glory to? How about when something bad happens?

16. Would you be accused as someone who prays too much and could they find evidence of that?

17. If you have been promoted on the job, was it because of your skills or God's gifts?

18. When you are thrown into the lion's den, how do you respond?

19. If an angel appeared to you, how would God describe you?

Chapter 14

NEHEMIAH AN EVERYDAY HERO FOR GOD

Nehemiah-Nehemiah, Ezra

Name NEHEMIAH - consolation; repentance of the Lord (from Hitchcock's Bible Names Dictionary,)
Heroic Traits: He knew how pray; he knew how to lead others; He had confidence in God; he was favored by God to succeed.
Mission: To rebuild the walls of Jerusalem and establish godly leadership.

Nehemiah Heroic Qualities to focus on in being an Everyday Hero:

- He was a mighty prayer warrior.
- He was a good, godly & strong leader.
- He served God and others.
- He was favored by God to succeed.

The Challenges Nehemiah Faced

- He faced distress, reproach, brokenness and scars.
- He was harassed by enemies that mocked, ridiculed and belittled his work and effort.
- He had to rebuild the walls of a city.
- He had to stick with his vision in the midst of opposition.

The Magnitude of Nehemiah's Task

- He was rebuilding a city that was destroyed.
- He had to face opposition with confidence and calm the people he was leading.
- He needed resources, time and people to do finish the work.
- He had to build and be ready to fight in a moment's notice.

While a cupbearer to the king of Persia, Nehemiah received news about the horrible condition of Jerusalem. The survivors of the captivity were in great distress and reproach. The wall of Jerusalem was also broken down and its gates burned with fire.

As you study the following qualities in Nehemiah, think about what God has put in you to be an everyday hero for God.

1.   Heroic Quality One – Nehemiah was a Prayer Warrior

We see Nehemiah's heart in communicating with God. He sat down, wept, mourned, fasted and prayed (Nehemiah 1:4). This was a man who knew how to pray - and he prayed often. It is important for you to make a habit of prayer. You can pray to God in times of trouble, darkness sorrow, and find answers from heaven. You can also pray just to connect and communicate with God.

An everyday hero is an everyday prayer warrior. **He prays with passion, power and his prayers produce positive results**. As Nehemiah prayed to God, God placed His plan in Nehemiah's heart (Nehemiah 2:12). God reveals His divine plans to a person who prays.

A true person of prayer prays in faith and remains confident in what was prayed long after the prayer is finished. If Nehemiah prayed for God to prosper him, then he needed to hold onto that point with great strength and declare what he prayed boldly (Nehemiah 1:11; 2:20). True and genuine prayer is followed by words that say the same truth as was said in the prayer. In other words, the words you speak when you pray should be the same words you speak after you have prayed.

Prayer is a powerful weapon in the hands of the faithful believer. Nehemiah prayed that his enemies would experience reproach and become plunder and be taken captive. He prayed that the iniquity of his enemies would be exposed because they angered the Lord (Nehemiah 4:4-5). Nehemiah's success came from the fact that he kept praying, "O God, strengthen my hands." (Nehemiah 6:9). God heard his prayer and gave him strength.

You can be an everyday hero as you develop your prayer life and connect with the Almighty God.

Heroic Characteristic of Prayer in the Scriptures

Powerful prayers are based on God's Word and build confidence in your heart. When you abide in God and His Words abide in you, you can ask what you will and it will be done by God (John 15:7; 1 John 5:14-15).

You pray to the Lord because He is your portion. He is everything you need, want and desire and in Him, you are not shaken. Prayer is a mighty weapon against; it is your *"spiritual air force"* that launches air strikes against evil. Keeping God's commands gets His attention when you pray. You should have a time of prayer every day (Ephesians 6:18; Psalm 102:17; 1 John 3:22; Acts 3:1).

Develop your prayer life and learn how to communicate with God to be an everyday hero.

2.   Heroic Quality Two – Nehemiah was a Strong Leader

Nehemiah was a leader because people followed him. He was able to influence many people in fulfilling God's purpose for His city. Together, he and his team rebuilt the walls of Jerusalem in fifty two days (Nehemiah 6:15). Nehemiah served and stood up for God's cause without compromising. He worked, worshiped and was willing and ready to fight, if necessary. He encouraged the people and protected them and the work. Under his leadership, a great task was completed very swiftly. He was able to influence a group of people in fulfilling God's purpose for His city. There were many people who helped him along the way.

Nehemiah was a man with a clear vision and he was able to communicate that vision for people to rally around and

work to bring it to pass (Nehemiah 2:17-18). People of influence, such as the King and Queen of Persia, supported Nehemiah's vision. They provided for him, protected him and promoted him (Nehemiah 1-9). He also led many social and political reforms among the people, including a return to pure worship and a renewed emphasis on true religion (Nehemiah Ch. 9).

Leaders are made by God and heroes rise to be leaders. God calls men and women to do great and small things for His kingdom. God called Nehemiah to rebuild the walls of Jerusalem like God called Moses to deliver the people of Israel from bondage. Nehemiah received his call through prayer and took his place as leader by becoming a Governor in Jerusalem (Nehemiah 1:1; 8:9; 10:1; 12:26, 47).

The world needs strong, godly leaders today; people who can hear from God; communicate a vision to people, and do what God commands; seek to fulfill His will. Nehemiah encountered opposition but he stood against his opponents with faith and courage (Nehemiah 2:10, 19).

Examples of Scorners

To scorn is to have contempt, disdain, dislike, disrespect and to disapprove. A scorner is a mocker who laughs at, despises and belittles anything that God does. Do not let a scorner stop you from doing what you are called to do (Nehemiah 2:19; Psalm 1:1).

Do not allow yourself to have contempt or disrespect for God or anything good. A scorner is one who: despises his boss; shows no honor to those in authority; makes light of people and makes them feel small; looks down on someone because of their age, race, gender or nationality and speaks prideful words that are lies against the righteous (*Nehemiah 2:19; Psalm 1:1; 31:18; Genesis 16:4; 1 Samuel 10:27; 14:11; 17:28, 42; Matthew 10:22; Hebrews 11:36-38*).

Nehemiah exemplified great strategy by setting people in the right place and right position to build with swords, spears, bows and tools (Nehemiah 4:13). He inspired his followers with encouraging words as he said, "*Do not be afraid of them. Remember the Lord, great and awesome and fight for your brethren, your sons, your daughters, your wives and your houses.*" (Nehemiah 4:14).

Nehemiah worked with the people and exemplified being a true servant leader (Nehemiah 4:23).

He confronted the nobles when he found out they were oppressing the people (Nehemiah 5:6-13).

He did not lay heavy burdens upon the people and he was very generous (Nehemiah 5:14-19).

He led the people in a spiritual reform to honor God and His word (Nehemiah Ch. 8). He withstood the attacks that came against him, the people and the work they were doing. He was a tough leader who overcame everything his enemies hurled at him and how they tried to harm him (Nehemiah 4:3; 6:2).

The builders worked with tools in one hand and weapons in the other (Nehemiah 4:17). To the taunts of his enemies, Nehemiah replied, "I am doing a great work, so that I cannot come down" He was not intimidated or moved by them (Nehemiah 6:3). Nothing could stop the project to rebuild the walls of Jerusalem (Nehemiah 2:10, 19; 6:1-14). You can be an everyday hero by not letting anything stop you from doing God's will!

Heroic Characteristic of Leadership in Scripture

Be an example to others in and show yourself a pattern of good works: (1 Timothy 4:12; Titus 2:7).

Follow this pattern to become a good leader.

A. **Word** – Know God's Word, understand it and live by every word in the Bible.

B. **Love** – Love God with all your heart and love people as yourself.

C. **Spirit** – Be zealous, passionate and compassionate for God.

D. **Faith** – Have the faith that comes from God and believe Him big and boldly.

E. **Purity** – Keep your heart pure, tender and sensitive to God's voice, heart and will.

F. **Read attentively** - Be encouraged in who you are in Christ and be teachable, continue to learn and study to show yourself approved to God a workman rightly dividing the truth.

G. **Continue to use, develop and increase your skill in the gifts that God has given you**.

H. **Meditate on these things** - Give yourself wholly to them and let others see your progress.

I. **Take heed to yourself** - Examine your heart and ways as you move forward on your journey with God. Be quick to forgive and quick to repent. Ask God for wisdom, understanding and help. Keep yourself on the right path and in the middle of the road. Do not ride the fence but get on the right side, God's side.

Has He called you to lead a group of people, to accomplish a task, or do something great? Learn His leadership principles and practice them in your life so you can be an everyday hero for God.

3. Heroic Quality Three – Nehemiah had Confidence in God

As mentioned, Nehemiah was a cup-bearer. He was an officer of high rank in royal courts, whose duty it was to serve the drinks at the royal table. On account of the constant fear of plots and intrigues against the king, a person must be regarded as thoroughly trustworthy to hold this position. He must guard against poison in the king's cup, and was sometimes required to swallow some of the wine before serving it. His confidential relations with the king often gave him a position of great influence. The position of cup bearer is greatly valued and given to only a select few throughout history. Qualifications for the job were not held lightly but of high esteem valued for their beauty and even more for their modesty, industriousness and courage (Wikipedia IBID).

Nehemiah's confidence in God made him a hero for God and to the people. He said to them, *"The God of heaven Himself will prosper us. Therefore we His servants will arise & build, but you have no heritage, right or memorial in Jerusalem."* (Nehemiah 2:20).

Ways in which Nehemiah showed confidence

- He showed uncompromising vigilance.
- He takes no notice of the serious charge brought against him.
- He claims he is sanctioned from the Most High to rebuild the city.
- He states clearly that he and his brethren will build as servants of the God of heaven.
- He meets opposition with defiance.
- He refuses to be intimidated by their scoffs or threats.
- He was confident in his prayer in when he asked God to prosper them.
- He was determined to build in spite of opposition, difficulties and discouragements.
- He did not divulge his plans and how he got to where he was to his mockers.
- He trusted God to prosper him, protect him and supply him with everything he needed.

Nehemiah confidently trusted in God. There were three main people who opposed the rebuilding of the wall of Jerusalem: Sanballat the Horonite (a Samaritan), Tobiah the Ammonite official, and Geshem the Arab (Nehemiah 2:10,19; 6:1-14).

Nehemiah answered his opposition with confident prayer. He prayed that God would put reproach on their enemies' heads; their opponents would be plundered and those who came against them would be judged for their sin (Nehemiah 4:4-5). An enemy who opposes God's hero, doing God's work, that enemy is opposing God. No matter how your enemy comes against you, keep doing what God called you to do and you will be an everyday hero!

Nehemiah showed confidence when attacked (Nehemiah Ch. 4).

There are things you can do to prepare to stand against a spiritual attack just like Nehemiah did. Pray to God because He listens when you pray in faith. Keep an eye on your work, your life, and your attitude day and night. Do not let your strength fail, but stay strong in God's Word and His Spirit. When people around you are speaking negative words, do not pay attention to them. Pay more attention to what God says about you than what they say against you.

Put people in the right positions in your life and in the work you are doing. Equip them with the right weapons and tools they need to fight and work. Speak encouraging words to those following you. Encourage them in the greater cause. Establish a way to communicate to your followers when to come together and fight. God makes you wiser than your enemies and He will fight for you.

Nehemiah showed confidence against Oppression (Nehemiah Ch. 5).

Nehemiah faced challenges and overcame them. There was a time when the people cried out due to low food supplies, deep debt, heavy taxes and being enslaved for their debts. There seemed to be no way out of this oppression.

The way the people were being treated angered Nehemiah. After he gave it some serious thought, he rebuked the nobles and leaders who were doing these things. Nehemiah lent the people money and grain and encouraged the rulers to stop charging their own people interest. He commanded that all the people's property be returned to them. The nobles heeded Nehemiah's commands and he set the reform in motion by getting the leaders to promise to his terms. He restored lands, vineyards, olive groves, houses and a 100th of the money, grain, new wine and oil. For twelve years he did not partake of the governor's provisions. Nehemiah shared with many people. The bondage was heavy on the people. Nehemiah asked God to look on what he did as a seed. Nehemiah was a wise and generous leader and delivered his people from oppression.

Develop your confidence in God and become fully persuaded in what He can do through you to be an everyday hero for God.

Nehemiah showed confidence against a conspiracy (Nehemiah Ch. 6).

Nehemiah's enemies heard that the wall was rebuilt without any breaks in it. They wanted to meet with Nehemiah to harm him. Nehemiah sent messengers to his opponents telling them about the great work that was being done and he should not leave the work.

Those who opposed the rebuilding of the wall tried four other times to trick Nehemiah into meeting with them and all four times he refused. Finally, his enemies sent a letter full of lies about what Nehemiah really intended to do. Nehemiah exposed the lies and asked God to strengthen his hands to work.

The enemies tried to get Nehemiah and the people to fear. You do not have to fear any enemy or what they attempt to do. Nehemiah stuck to his work and finished the wall in record time, fifty-two days. When the wall was finished their enemies were disheartened, lost confidence and knew God was in this work. Be confident in God above anyone that conspires against you.

4.   **Heroic Quality Four – Nehemiah had God's favor to succeed.**

Nehemiah was commissioned by God to rebuild the wall of Jerusalem. **God gave Nehemiah his favor to accomplish his great task**. God's favor brought to Nehemiah divine protection, provision and permission to do what God wanted him to do with excellence (Nehemiah 1:2-9).

Nehemiah testified to the high ranking Israelites, the priests, nobles and officials that God's hand was on him. **Favor occurs when God places His hands on you** (Nehemiah 2:18). Also, God brought their enemies plot to nothing and the work was not interrupted (Nehemiah 4:15).

Finally, God's favor worked in such a way that He strengthened the people and they finished the project in fifty-two days (Nehemiah 6:15). Everything they needed was provided. No one was injured and the work was completed with God's favor.

The Heroic Characteristic of Favor in the Scriptures

Favor comes from God and enables the one who receives it to accomplish great things. Jesus grew in wisdom, stature and favor with God and man. God's favor can be on you throughout your life. A good man obtains favor from the Lord. The Lord will surround the righteous with favor like a shield. If you walk with God, you can obtain favor from Him (Luke 2:52; Psalm 30:5; 5:12; Proverbs 12:2; 8:35)

A person with good understanding gains favor from the Lord. Even Mary, the mother of Jesus, found favor with God. Favor is found at God's throne. God's favor worked in the early church and caused the gospel to flourish (Proverbs 13:15; Luke 1:30; Acts 2:42; Hebrews 4:16).

You can get favor from the Lord also and be an everyday hero for Him. To better understand the heroic qualities that Nehemiah possessed and how he used them, consider answering the following questions honestly and sincerely. Be willing to make any adjustments in your heart and life to improve your skills as a godly hero.

Questions to consider for your personal growth about being an everyday hero like Nehemiah

1. What touches your heart?

2. How effective are your prayers? Do they produce the results you desire and bring you closer to God?

3. What work, project, event or people has God called you to get involved with?

4. How has the favor of God operated in your life to help you accomplish what God has called you to do?

5. What kind of opposition have you encountered in endeavoring to follow God's plan for your life?

6. Who do you have helping you accomplish what God has called you to do?

7. What kind of changes have you made in yourself and your life to do God's will?

8. What have you accomplished for God and how long did it take to complete it?

9. If God were to write a book about your life what do you think He would say about you?

Chapter 15

PAUL AN EVERYDAY HERO FOR GOD

PAUL – Acts and New Testament

Name: PAUL – Paul small; little   (from Hitchcock's Bible Names Dictionary)

Heroic Traits: His real zeal, his powerful vision, his strong courage and his intense earnestness.

Mission: Paul was a chosen vessel for God to bear the Lord's name before Gentiles, kings and the children of Israel. He was going to suffer for the Lord's name sake.

Paul's Heroic Qualities to focus on in being an Everyday Hero:

- Paul had a zeal for people to be born again since his life changed so drastically.
- Paul had several visions in his life which he carried out fully.
- Paul was bold & courageous in facing tests, trials, kings, Gentiles and Israel.
- Paul had a focused intensity on him that caused him to do a great work for God.

The Challenges Paul Faced

- His entire theology was overturned when Jesus met him on the road to Damascus.
- He was shown by God how much he would suffer for obeying God.
- He was blind for three days as he considered whether or not to obey & answer God's call.
- He was persecuted harshly and faced many perilous things.
- He had to face kings, Gentiles and his countrymen.

The Magnitude of Paul's Task

- He was preaching the gospel and establishing churches where none existed.
- He would become a church planter and what God showed him would minister to generations.
- He would end up writing about half of the New Testament & laying the foundation of church life.
- He would spend his time traveling the known world to preach the gospel.

1. Heroic Quality One - Paul had an earnest zeal for God.

To have zeal, is to possess great energy or enthusiasm in pursuit of a cause or an objective. When you are zealous, you have a strong feeling of interest that makes you very eager and determined to do something. Zeal encourages focused discipline in daily obedience to God's will. Passion, fire, fervor and devotion are relatives of zeal.

To be earnest is to have a serious intention, purpose or effort. An earnest man shows depth and sincerity of feeling and what he does demands serious attention free from jesting. Paul writes in Romans 12:11-16, *"Do not lag in diligence; be fervent in spirit; serve the Lord; rejoice in hope; be patient in tribulation; continue steadfast in prayer."*

Paul was a man of great passion. Before he met Christ, he had a great passion for the law and Judaism. He carried out terrifying tasks of arresting Christians, imprisoning them, persecuting them and even witnessing their death. His actions gave him a reputation that people feared. Paul proved an apt pupil in the religion of Judaism. He outstripped many of his fellow students in his enthusiasm for ancestral traditions and in his zeal for the Jewish law. This zeal found a ready outlet in his assault on the infant church of Jerusalem.

Paul was zealous for the wrong things when he was younger. Paul testified himself how he persecuted God's church to an extreme degree and advanced in Judaism beyond many of his contemporaries. He was very zealous (Galatians 1:13-14). He persecuted the early Christian church; he entered their houses; he dragged Christian men and women to prison and he consented to and witnessed their deaths (Acts 8:3; 7:58; 9:1).

As zealous as Paul was to excel in Judaism and persecute Christians, he **became extremely zealous in serving God the right way**. God used Paul's zeal and used it for His glory. No matter what you have done, God can really turn things around for you. Paul was so powerfully transformed that people who knew him were amazed (Acts 9:19-23). Paul was a blasphemer, a persecutor and an arrogant man and by God's grace, he became an apostle, a preacher and a missionary who wrote about half of the New Testament (1 Timothy 1:13).

Paul's zeal was seen in how boldly he spoke about the Lord and debated with opposing groups. He earnestly focused on finishing his course and assignment in ministry (Acts 9:28; 20:24). God used Paul to start many churches and often he warned them for long periods of time in tears. He was very passionate to see his fellow Israelites become born again and he was willing to become all things to all people so some would know Jesus as Lord (Acts 20:31; 21:13; 22:3-5; Romans 9:3-4; 1 Corinthians 9:19-23).

Paul was consumed with zeal and was willing to die for what he believed in. His zeal caused him to be spiritually, emotionally and physically involved in his work. What he wrote to the churches was weighty and powerful. His passion kept him doing what he was called to do even though he faced beatings, imprisonments and many dangers. He would labor night and day so that he would not be a burden to the churches he started and encouraged (Acts 21:13; 2 Corinthians 2:4; 10:10; 11:23-27; 1 Thessalonians 2:9).

Heroic Characteristic of Zeal in Scripture

A zealous person finds something to do and does it mightily.

He does not fear or let his hands become weak. A person with passion works his vision, and a person without passion does nothing. Zeal is a compelling force that moves you to do God's will. You need zeal to be an edifying encourager (Ecclesiastes 9:10; Zephaniah 3:16-17; Haggai 2:4-7; Luke 14:23-24; 1 Corinthians 14:12).

It is hard to stop a zealous man for he is steadfast, immovable and abounding in the Lord's work. It is good to be man with zeal. Stir up the gifts that are in you because a zealous man is a stirred man. Let people see your zeal in proclaiming truth; being prepared; persuading others; correcting them and encouraging them with all longsuffering and teaching (1 Corinthians 15:58; Galatians 4:18; 2 Timothy 1:6; 4:2; 2 Corinthians 9:2; Colossians 4:13; 2 Peter 1:13).

The opposite of zeal is to be sluggish. As a zealous person, you take initiative and labor until the work is completed. Choose to let zeal and passion consume you. The Father's business needs you to be a zealous worker. Do God's will with great passion and make it more important than eating food (Hebrews 6:12; Nehemiah 4:21; 2 Chronicles 29:34; Psalm 119:139; John 2:17; Luke 2:49; John 4:34).

When God gives you an assignment carry it out fervently. The prophet Elisha encouraged Joash, King of Israel to strike the ground with an arrow to symbolize the defeat of the Syrians. He only struck the ground three times. Elisha was angry with his lack of zeal and told him he should have struck the ground five or six times to completely destroy his enemy. Zeal puts you over the top (2 Kings 13:14-21).

Become passionate and zealous about God's will in your life and be an everyday hero for Him.

2. Heroic Quality Two – Paul was a man of Great Vision

Visions are pictures that reveal divine insight into God's plan: a vision is a supernatural appearance.

Strong's dictionary defines it as: spiritual seeing; to be seen; an appearing; the act of exhibiting oneself to view; A sight, a vision, an appearance presented to one whether asleep or awake (Strong's IBID).

Paul's Visions

1. Paul's Vision of Christ   (Act 9:3-6; 26:13-15)
- A Hero needs a good vision to go in the right direction. God led Paul step by step through visions, His presence and His Word. God revealed truth to Paul through the visions.
    - a. While Paul was threatening & murdering the disciples of the Lord on his way to Damascus, the Lord appeared to him.
    - b. Christ revealed Himself to Paul through a vision. This vision brought him to Christ. God brought Paul into heaven's light and out of the darkness and blindness.
    - c. The Lord instructed Paul to go into the city and wait until he was told what he must do.
    - d. The men traveling with Paul heard the voice but saw no one (Acts 9:7)
    - e. Paul was blind for three days after the vision. He fasted and probably prayed.
    - f. God prepared Paul for Ananias to come and lay his hands on him (Acts 9:12)

2. Paul's Missionary Vision (Acts 16:9)
-
    - a. The Holy Spirit forbade Paul and his team to preach in Asia and Bithynia (Acts 16:6)
    - b. While in Troas, Paul had a vision of a man from Macedonia standing & pleading with him to come to Macedonia. God led Paul to the place He wanted him to be (Acts 16:9)
    - c. Paul and his team left Troas, went to Samothrace, and the next day came to Neapolis. From there they went to Philippi & stayed there some days all as a result of the vision.

3. Paul's Vision of Encouragement   (Acts 18:9)

a. The Lord spoke to Paul at night in a vision saying, "Do not be afraid, but speak and do not keep silent (Acts 18:9)

b. The Lord said He was with Paul and no one would attack him or hurt him. The Lord had many people in Corinth that were ripe recipients of the gospel. Paul stayed there a year and six months.

4. **Paul's Vision of Warning** (Acts 22:12-21)
   a. Paul recounts his experience with the Lord and when Ananias came to lay his hands on him.
   b. While Paul was praying in the temple in Jerusalem, he was in a trance (Acts 22:17)
   c. The Lord warned Paul to leave Jerusalem quickly, for the people would not receive the truth about Him. Jesus told Paul that He would send him to the Gentiles (Acts 22:18)

5. **Paul's Vision of Rome**   (Acts 23:10-13)
   a. The Lord stood by Paul at night and said, "Be of good cheer, Paul; for as you have testified for Me in Jerusalem, so you must also bear witness at Rome." (Acts 23:11)
   b. At this time, a group of forty Jews banded together & committed to kill Paul (Acts 23:12)

6. **Paul's Vision of Rescue**   (Acts 27:20-32)
   a. An angel stood by Paul, encouraged him not to fear, told him he must be brought before Caesar and gave God's Word that no life would be lost (Acts 27:23). God gave Paul a personal touch, called him by name, stood by him in his darkest moment, encouraged him and revealed to him His divine plan & purpose of his life.
   b. Paul believed just as it was spoken to him by the angel. This vision made Paul bold and gave him a voice on the ship (Acts 27:30-31).The sailors were going to leave the ship, but Paul said to the centurion that the men must stay with the ship to live. The soldiers heeded Paul's words and cut the ropes of smaller boats.

c. Paul took communion – he took bread, gave thanks to God, broke it and ate it (Acts 27:35)

d. There were 276 people on the ship (Acts 27:37). God's Word proved true as all on the ship made it to land (Acts 27:44)

7. **Paul's Vision of Paradise** (2 Corinthians 12:1-4)

a. Paul speaks of visions & revelations of the Lord which could have taken place shortly after his conversion and encounter with Ananias (Acts 22:17)

b. Paul did not know if he was out of body or in his body in heaven. He was caught up to God's dwelling place, the seat of the divine Majesty, and the residence of the holy angels (Deuteronomy 10:14; Psalm 148:4; Ephesians 4:10)

c. While Paul was there, he heard inexpressible words (2 Corinthians 12:4)

    i. *"I was caught up to paradise and heard things so astounding that they cannot be expressed in words, things no human is allowed to tell."* NLT

    ii. *"I was snatched away to Paradise and heard things that cannot be expressed in words, things that no human being has a right even to mention."* ISV

    iii. *"I was caught up into paradise and heard things too sacred to be put into words, things that a person is not permitted to speak."* NET Bible

    iv. *"That he was caught up into paradise, and heard secret words, which it is not granted to man to utter."* Douay-Rheims Bible

    v. *"That he was caught away to the paradise, and heard unutterable sayings, that it is not possible for man to speak."* YLT

Paul's Obedience to these visions   (Acts 26:19)

• Obedience to God-given visions is the key to being an everyday hero for God. Some people are prophetic and they are visual learners. Paul certainly saw many things and acted on all that he saw. Paul took the visions he had and ran with them to fulfill them. He also used his vision to encourage and inspire others.

    d. Paul reiterates his vision to King Agrippa. Paul is testifying before a king just as God said he would when he was saved (Acts 9:15-16; 26:12-19).

    e. Paul obeyed the heavenly vision and began preaching in Damascus, then Jerusalem, in all Judea and to the Gentiles (Acts 26:19)

    f. Paul considered himself a master builder of the church. He would lay the foundation by starting churches then turn them over to pastors who continued to build on the foundation that was laid by Paul (1 Corinthians 3:10-12).

    g. Paul acknowledged that God helped him faithfully in his journeys (Acts 26:22)

    h. King Agrippa was almost persuaded to become a Christian (Acts 26:28)

Let God give you a vision, a direction and a plan for your life so you can be an everyday hero for God.

3. Heroic Quality Three – Paul Displayed Bold Courage in Facing Tests and Trials before Kings, Gentiles and Israel.

A Hero will be tested so his boldness and courage can rise up and be strong. Only a hero will be bold and courageous when tests and trials come. You can be bold and courageous also to be an everyday hero for God.

- Paul boldly proclaimed Christ as Messiah, grew in skill and confounded the Jews (Acts 9:19-22)
- Barnabas testified to the church that Paul spoke boldly in the name of Jesus (Acts 9:27-30)
- Paul preached the gospel unashamedly, confronted a sorcerer and won (Acts 13:6-12)
- Paul and Barnabas boldly resisted becoming objects of worship by the people (Acts 14:14-19)

- After being stoned and left for dead, Paul went back into the city where the stoning occurred (Acts 14:20)
- Paul risked his life to preach the gospel to the world (Acts 15:25-26)
- Paul & Silas boldly praised God at midnight from a dungeon and in chains (Acts 16:25-31)
- Paul was courageous to use his citizenship when necessary (Acts 16:35-40)
- Paul boldly proclaimed the gospel wherever he went every day (Acts 17:16-33)
- Paul was courageous because he knew that God's presence was with him (Acts 18:9)
- Paul was not afraid to stand up for himself and declare the truth boldly (Acts 24:13-21)

The Heroic Characteristic of Boldness and Courage in the Scriptures

- Peter and John displayed bold courage in raising the lame man at the gate called Beautiful. Other people recognized their boldness came from being with Jesus (Acts 4:13). They did not back down nor compromise what they believed to be true. The proof of God's power was in the man who was healed.

-
    - Joseph of Arimathea boldly appeared before Pilate and asked for Jesus' body (Matthew 15:43)
    - The early church prayed and proclaimed courageously and the building shook (Acts 4:31)
    - Paul preached fearlessly, effectively persuading Jews about God's kingdom (Acts 19:8)
    - Having great hope enables you to be bold in your speech (2 Corinthians 3:12)
    - A godly hero can approach God's throne boldly and confidently (Hebrews 4:16)

Step out boldly and do something for the Lord to become an everyday hero for God.

4. Heroic Quality Four – Paul was Focused, Intense and Unstoppable in his Obedience.

An intense man speaks in a loud voice; is important and distinguished; demonstrates strength, power potency and ferocity. He has exceptionally great concentration or force. He shows a high degree of emotional excitement and depth of feeling.

Paul was an intense and powerful force for the Lord, and he did a great work for God's kingdom. He started many churches. As a starter, Paul needed these qualities to create something from the ground up. Paul considered himself to be a wise master builder, who established churches where there were no churches (1 Corinthians 3:10). Every godly hero needs to be focused, intense and unstoppable.

Paul responded and embraced God's call quickly to go and preach the gospel. He was a missionary, an apostle and a tent maker. God used him to write about half of the New Testament. In doing great exploits for God, he was disciplined and often paid his own way, by making tents. He suffered great persecution in preaching the gospel and standing strong for what he believed in. He never quit (Acts 9:20; 1 Corinthians 9:15-27; 2 Corinthians 11:22-33).

Paul was so intense that he said he had joy in all his afflictions. That is intense! Paul is like an athlete in extreme sports, he took Christianity and ministry to the extreme! (2 Corinthians 7:4-10)

Paul was put in prison many times yet he considered his imprisonment to advance the gospel. He encouraged people to follow his example and told them not to let his chains and imprisonments hinder them (Philippians 1:12-13; 4:9; 1 Thessalonians 2:10).

One of Paul's heroic qualities was his focused intensity by which he served God. You can also be an everyday hero for God by becoming more intense and focused. Let God fill you and consume you. Display God's character, love and faith, embrace His call for your life and go and do what God said. Focus on doing

God's will for your life, be intense and unstoppable, and become and everyday hero for God!

To help you understand Paul's heroic qualities he possessed and how he used them to be an everyday hero, consider the following questions and answer them sincerely and make any adjustments or corrections that you need to make to be a godly hero.

Questions to consider for your personal growth about being an everyday hero like Paul

1. How diligent of a person are you? Do you finish what you start or do you leave many things undone?

2. Are you passionate about God, His Word and accomplishing His will for your life? How would others know you are a passionate person in the things of God?

3. How would people who know you describe what you are passionate about?

4. What extreme measures would you take to help another person know the Lord?

5. What is the vision for your life? Describe some things that God has shown you recently.

6. What were some tests you faced? How well did you do in passing those tests?

7. Have you ever suffered for the sake of the gospel? If not, why do you think that is? If yes, describe what you were feeling and how you were treated.

8. Have you ever had to stand up for what you believed publicly? What was that like?

9. What are some things you could do to become more focused and a greater force for God?

10. Could you boldly say to others, "Follow my example."? If not, what would you change?

Chapter 16

PETER AN EVERYDAY HERO FOR GOD

Peter – The gospels, Acts and 1 & 2 Peter

Name: A rock or stone   (from Hitchcock's Bible Names Dictionary)

Heroic Traits: Action-oriented; Spiritual insight; Leadership; Unwillingness to quit

Mission: He was to follow Christ, be a fisher of men and a preacher of the gospel of Christ.

> *"They detached from their sphere of interests and attached to Jesus as their leader. Jesus would change their character which was necessary for this new type of fishing. Fishing requires care, patience, skill, endurance and better habits in life."*
> *(Pulpit Commentary)*

> *"Now leave your ordinary employments, and become my constant attendants; that by continually hearing my doctrine, and seeing my miracles, you may be fitted, in due time, to become my messengers to mankind. You shall gather men into the gospel net, and gain them over to the faith. They straightway left their nets and followed him — Influenced by the power of his word, and struck with the wonderful miracle recorded (Luke 5:6-9)"*
>   *(Meyer's NT Commentary)*

Peter's Heroic Qualities that made him an Everyday Hero:

- Peter was action-oriented. Peter took action when others did not. God turned Peter's negative actions into positive actions. A hero needs to be able to take action quickly.

- Peter had great spiritual insight in recognizing truth and receiving revelation from heaven.
- Peter was a leader in disguise. As God worked in him he became a great champion for God, the church and winning the lost. He grew in the knowledge of God and became a mighty man.
- Peter was unwilling to quit even though he denied knowing Christ. He had one of the greatest comebacks ever from denying knowing Christ to preaching on the day of Pentecost.

The Challenges Peter Faced:

- Peter was a fisherman who was skilled at catching fish. He was not a trained preacher to deliver God's message to the masses.
- Peter was not highly educated as stated by the Sanhedrin in Acts 4:13. His being with Jesus overrode any deficiency in education.
- Peter had to use his fishing skills to now influence men and women to receive Christ as Savior. He changed careers very quickly.
- Peter had to overcome many misspoken words and awkward actions that Jesus had to correct. He never let his mistakes keep him down for long. He kept getting up and progressing forward.
- He moved from the fish of the sea to the people of the land. He went from a boat to a platform.

The Magnitude of Peter's Task:

- Peter had a wife and family. How would he take care of his family now that he left his fishing business?
- How would God turn a fisherman into a preacher to deliver the greatest message of all time?
- Peter would now be working directly with people in a different capacity- to lead them to Christ.

- Peter was called to leave something he knew and enter into something he did not know.

1. Heroic Quality One – Peter was Action-Oriented

You may have heard of the term *"action heroes"*. A hero needs to be a man of action. He takes action when others are in danger or when others cannot or will not act. Peter was a man who took action, even though at times, it was the wrong action to take. Peter acted when others remained still.

The first action that Peter took was to immediately surrender his life to Jesus when he encountered Him by the sea. Jesus asked Peter to follow Him, and Peter did without hesitation (Matthew 4:18-20). In another account, Jesus borrowed Peter's boat, preached a message and told Peter to launch his nets into the deep for a great catch. Peter, who was tired from working all night and caught nothing, obeyed the Lord's Words and cast his net into the water. The catch of fish was so amazing and overwhelming that Peter humbled himself before Jesus and committed his life to following Him whole-heartedly (Luke 5:1-11)

Another action Peter took was to step out of the boat and walk on water. That was something that no other disciple of Jesus did. The disciples saw Jesus walking on the water at night and they thought it was a ghost. Jesus spoke to them and told them not to fear but be of good cheer. Peter said, "If that is you Jesus, ask me to come to you." Jesus said, "Come!" This statement applied to any person that was in the boat. Anyone could have responded and walked on the water but **only Peter did**. He alone stepped out of the boat and walked on the water. Even though he didn't make it all the way to Jesus, he did act on His Word. This made Peter a hero for God (Matthew 14:28-33).

One of Peter's encounters with the Lord occurred on a mountain where Peter and two other disciples saw Jesus in His full glory. While they were there with Jesus, He was transformed in front of them. His face shone like the sun and His clothes became white as snow. As Peter witnessed this, his first response was that he said that it was good for them to be there. He wanted to act and make three tents for Moses and Elijah who also appeared with Jesus (Matthew 17:1-10).

Peter was always drawn to Jesus. With all his ups and downs, he always found his way to Jesus. After Jesus rose from the dead, Peter told the disciples that he was going fishing. Many of the disciples joined him. They fished at night and caught nothing. Jesus showed up on the shore, but the disciples did not recognize Him. He asked those in the boat if they had any food or caught any fish. When they told Him no, Jesus told them to cast the net on the other side of the boat. They could barely bring the net in because it was so full. John told Peter it was the Lord. Peter jumped in the water and swam to shore to be with Jesus (John 21:1-19).

The Heroic Characteristic of being Action-Oriented in Scripture

God wants you to be a man of action and do what He says. If you confess that Jesus is your Lord then you must do what His Word says. The Pharisees were leaders in the religion of Judaism. Many of them believed in Jesus; but because they loved the praise of men more than the approval of God, they **did not confess** Jesus as their Lord. They did not act on what they believed and did not benefit from God's best gift. Not acting the right way can be a costly mistake (James 1:22; Matthew 7:21-29; 12:50; Luke 6:46-49; John 12:42-43).

If you hear what God says, **you are not blessed until you act on or act out what you heard**. Actions begin with thoughts. You should think about God, His Kingdom, and His Word and how you can do what He says to do. **Everything you do should bring glory and honor to Jesus**. If you know that you should do something good and you do not do it, it is sin (Romans 2:13; Philippians 4:8-9; Colossians 3:17; James 4:17; 1 John 2:3)

Listen to what the Lord says and do it immediately to become an everyday hero for God.

2. Heroic Quality Two – Peter had Great Spiritual Insight that made him a Hero

Peter was a rough and tough fisherman whose education was less than a college graduate. When the lame man was healed at the temple, the people noticed the courage of Peter and John and **realized they were unschooled and ordinary men**. The miracle was so astonishing that the people also realized these men had been with Jesus. You may not have a degree from a college or university but if you spend time with Jesus you will learn much and do a lot (Acts 4:13).

Peter was a disciple of Jesus, who was taught and trained by Him. Jesus taught Peter how to catch men. God revealed truths to Peter that were so profound, they could not come from anyone else. When Peter shared his insights with others they were amazed. Peter knew that Jesus was the Christ because God revealed that truth to him (Matthew 16:13-20).

Jesus recognized that His Father in heaven had revealed this truth to Peter. Peter did not come to this realization through education, any person or any natural means. This truth was revealed to Peter from heaven. **It showed the insight that Peter had and it demonstrated the power of revelation**. You can know things by divine revelation better than learning them or experiencing them. Jesus told Peter that He was going to build His church on the revelation of truth. Knowing who Jesus is, is the foundation upon which Jesus is building His church.

Peter saw unique truth in Jesus. He noticed His manner, His speech and the way He did things. Peter would not have followed Jesus so quickly had he not saw something unique, special and different from the world. Jesus walked by Peter and said, "Follow

Me." Peter responded by laying his nets down and following Jesus (Matthew 4:18; Mark 1:16-20; Luke 5:1-11).

Peter was close to Jesus and was privileged to be in places the other disciples were not. **Peter, along with James and John, saw Jesus in His full glory** as Jesus was transformed before their eyes on a mountain. Peter thought this was a good place to be because he had a glimpse of God's glory (Matthew 17:1-13).

Peter had the privilege of praying with Jesus in His most trying moment in the garden Gethsemane (Matthew 26:37-45). Peter also accompanied Jesus into the room where Jairus' daughter was raised from the dead (Mark 5:37). **These experiences gave Peter insight into who Jesus was** and I am sure that they were the reasons he came back to Jesus after he denied him.

When Jesus preached about eating His flesh and drinking His blood many people turned away from following Him. He was not saying this in a literal sense - it has a vast spiritual significance. So many people stopped following Jesus that He asked His twelve closest followers if they wanted to leave Him also.

Peter spoke up and declared, "Lord, to whom shall we go? You have the words of eternal life and we believe and know that You are the Christ, the Son of the living God!" (John 6:65-69)

Peter had great insight to who Jesus was. Do you have insight into who Jesus is to you? Continue to develop your insight into spiritual truths to become and everyday hero.

The Heroic Characteristic of Spiritual Insight in the Scriptures

Divine insight increases your knowledge, wisdom and understanding which enhances your faith. Ask the Lord to open your eyes and increase your understanding so you can know the great things He has given to you. Jesus will help you understand and comprehend His hidden truths. God's Word is a light that makes darkness flee from your life (Ephesians 1:18-19; Luke 24:45; John 12:46).

Jesus teaches you what is true about God the Father. Turning to the Lord causes the veil covering your heart to be removed. God's Word shines in your heart to give you the light of knowledge of God's glory (John 15:15; 2 Corinthians 3:15; 4:6).

Pray to God and ask Him to show you things about Him, His kingdom and your purpose. He will show you wonderful things so you can be an everyday hero for God.

3. Heroic Quality Three – Peter became an Influential Leader in the Church

God did an amazing work in Peter's life. Peter was restored by Jesus and He commanded him to go and feed God's sheep, and become the leader God called him to be (John 21:15-19). He initiated the process to choose Judas' replacement (Acts 1:14-26). As a leader, you instruct, instill and initiate change.

When God poured out His Spirit upon all flesh, Peter was baptized with the Holy Ghost and fire. **This baptism empowered him, emboldened him and enabled him to speak powerfully to a huge crowd**. This is a dramatic and positive change that took place in Peter's heart. Once again, we see **Peter standing up for the Lord, raising his voice and preaching** the first message on the day of Pentecost (Acts Ch. 2).

Peter was taking his place to be the leader God had called and created him to be. **Believers could look to Peter and see him take charge of situations and act boldly, confidently and powerfully** because He was leading like God made him to lead. Under his leadership, three thousand people were born again and added to the church all in one service. That is amazing! (Acts 2:41).

In Acts Ch. 3, the Bible tells us about a lame man at the gate called Beautiful. That man would sit there begging people for money as they entered the temple. Peter captured this man's attention saying, "Look at us!" The man looked at them expectantly. Peter declared he did not have any money but such as he had, he gave to the man. Peter took him by the hand and commanded him to rise and walk. The man's legs were strengthened and he leaped up, stood and walked. Peter and John were not ashamed, embarrassed or worried about this public miracle that God did on the way to pray.

What made Peter a great leader? The answer is: **he spent time with Jesus**. The Sanhedrin professed that Peter and John were untrained and unlearned men. Yet, their bold speech and actions demonstrated that they had been with Jesus. Peter and John were not intimidated or fearful; **they were bold lions who testified about Jesus and demonstrated His power publicly**. Even when they were commanded not to speak in the name of Jesus and were threatened with physical harm, they refused to back down or to do what man said they should do (Acts Ch. 4).

Peter was a strong leader and kept people accountable to God's Word and Spirit. A couple, Ananias and his wife Sapphira, conspired together to lie to God about an offering they gave to the church. By publicly declaring they were giving the full amount of money and secretly, they were keeping a portion of it for themselves, they lied to the church and to God.

Peter was a strong leader because he confronted the evil this couple did, he called their bluff and exposed their lie. He rebuked them publicly and recognized it was the devil who influenced them to lie to God. Nothing gets by God! God's holiness needed to be seen. Both Ananias and his wife Sapphira dropped dead in church. They were offered mercy had they acknowledged their sin and repented; they refused to do both; they died and probably ended up in hell. **Good leaders adhere to God's standards and keep others accountable to them** (Acts Ch. 5).

The Heroic Characteristic of Leadership in the Scriptures

As a leader, you are an example for others to follow. People should follow your leadership only as you follow Christ.

Leadership was meant to be duplicated and modeled. Followers become like their leaders in many ways by sharing the same nature, heart; attitude and cause. The quality of your leadership will be determined by the quality of your character which is to be holy, righteous and blameless (1 Timothy 4:12-16; 1 Corinthians 11:1; 1 Thessalonians 1:6-7; 2:10-12).

A leader needs to accomplish a vision that is be achieved with diligence and zeal. Your vision will not be accomplished if you are idle or lazy. As a leader, you are an example to others in what you do, what you say and how trustworthy you are. Pattern your life after Jesus, the greatest and most effective Leader of all time, by doing what He did, saying what He said and treating people like He treated them (2 Thessalonians 3:6-10; Titus 2:6-8; John 3:6-10).

God has called you to lead, so step up and rely on God to give you wisdom, strength and power to be an everyday hero for God!

4. Heroic Quality Four – Peter was Unwilling to Quit

A very important quality that every hero must possess is a strong determination to accomplish goals and never quit. Refuse to let anyone or anything stop you from doing what God wants you to do. Even when you miss it and make a mistake do not quit. Get up and go on!

Peter demonstrated his unwillingness to quit when he returned to Jesus after he made a grave mistake and denied knowing Jesus. Jesus told Peter that Satan wanted to sift him as wheat. When you sift wheat you separate the good part from the bad. Satan wanted to separate Peter from Jesus and trample him under his feet (Luke 22:31-34).

Jesus knows what Satan is going to do before he does it. The Lord prepares you by: warning you; getting your attention to draw close to Him and avoiding the traps that the enemy has set. Jesus informed Peter that He prayed specifically that Peter's faith should not fail. Jesus expected Peter to return to Him and when Peter returned, he went and strengthened the brethren. Jesus knew Peter would fall, but He also was persuaded that Peter would return (Luke 22:31-32).

Peter responded to Jesus' warning with arrogance and stated that he was ready to go with Jesus to prison and die for Him. Peter wanted to look strong in front of Jesus and the other disciples, but Jesus knows the hearts of men He knew what was in Peter's heart. The attitude in his heart was different from the words he said in front of his peers and Jesus (Luke 22:33).

Peter denied knowing the Lord three times: once to a servant girl; once to another girl; once to a crowd that was gathered by a fire. Peter denied knowing Jesus and having a relationship with Him so vehemently, that he began to curse and swear at the people. His last statement about Jesus before the rooster crowed was, "*I do not know the man.*" Peter heard the rooster crow, he left and wept bitterly (Matthew 26:69-76; Mark 14:66-72; Luke 22:54-62; John 18:15-18, 25-27).

Peter made an incredible and historical comeback after messing up majorly relying only on his natural strength. He was with the disciples when Jesus rose from the dead; and he was the first person that Mary Magdalene told about Jesus' empty tomb. Peter ran to the tomb and was the first one to enter (John 20:1-7).

After Jesus had risen from the dead, Peter went fishing and some of the disciples went with him. They fished all night and caught nothing. Early in the morning, Jesus stood on the shore and asked those in the boat if they had caught anything. They told him that they did not catch anything. He told them to throw their net on the right side for a great catch. The men in the boat could hardly pull the net in being so full. It was apparent to them the man on the shore was the Lord. When Peter heard that, he jumped in the water and swam to Jesus (John Ch. 21).

When Peter came to Jesus, Jesus asked Peter if he loved Him more than anyone. Peter said yes. Jesus asked this question of Peter three times, perhaps to override the three denials. Here,

Peter declared his love for the Lord and he was fully restored, forgiven and cleansed for his denial. His ministry began at the sea and he was restored at the sea (John 21:15-23).

Peter went on to preach on the day of Pentecost and became a great and solid leader in the church. God worked great miracles through Peter that changed atmospheres and cities. This is one of the great comebacks which made Peter a hero for God (Acts Ch. 2).

Think about things that you have had to overcome. You are more than a conqueror through Christ Jesus and can do all things through Christ who strengthens you! Keep overcoming and running to the Lord no matter what to be an everyday hero for God.

The Heroic Characteristic of Great Comebacks in the Scriptures

- The prodigal son went from sin, to the pig pen, and returned home (Luke 15:13-24)
- Lazarus resurrected to life after being dead four days when Jesus called him out (John Ch. 11)
- Zacchaeus changed from being a greedy, covetous, cheating man, into one who repented, was generous and received eternal life (Luke 19:1-10)
- For thirty-eight years, a sick man sat by a pool waiting for something to happen to him. One meeting with Jesus changed him from being sick to healed (John 5:1-15)
- A woman had an issue of blood twelve years until she touched Jesus, then she stopped bleeding and was completely healed (Mark 5:21-32)
- A woman could not stand up straight because she had a spirit of infirmity for eighteen years in her until Jesus came to her church and set her completely free (Luke 13:10-17)

You have not gotten too far away from God. He can save you, deliver you, heal and help you. Follow him back and be an everyday hero for God. To help you understand the heroic qualities that Peter possessed and used to become a godly hero, consider the following questions and answer them sincerely and make adjustments as needed.

Questions to consider for your personal growth about being an everyday hero like Peter

1. How have you acted on God's word recently? What steps have you taken to do what God has spoken to you?

2. What hinders you from obeying quickly the things that God has spoken to you? How do you deal with hindrances?

3. What have you discovered in God's word recently? How often do you see things you have never seen before?

4. What are some experiences or encounters you have had with the Lord? How did they help you?

5. How has your understanding of God's truths increased? How did that new understanding change you?

6. What has God called you to lead? What are you doing to develop your leadership skills?

7. Who would you consider to be a mentor in your life? How often do you hear them or see them?

8. Would you feel comfortable if people chose to follow your example?

9. What are some challenges or setbacks you have had to overcome? How did you overcome them?

Chapter 17

TIMOTHY AN EVEYDAY HERO FOR GOD

Timothy – Acts, 1 & 2 Timothy and New Testament

Name: [TIM uh thih] Honored of God   (from Nelson's Illustrated Bible Dictionary)
Heroic Traits: Rich Faith; A Good Worker; Proven Character; Godly Encouragement.
Mission: Timothy was called by God to be a missionary, strengthen churches and be a pastor.

Timothy was well spoken of by the brethren in Lystra and Iconium. As he traveled with Paul to the different places, the churches were strengthened in the faith and increased in number daily (Acts 16:2-5).

Timothy's Heroic Qualities to focus on in being an Everyday Hero:

- Timothy was rich in faith as it was taught by his grandmother Lois and his mother Eunice.
- Timothy was a good worker and served in many different capacities for God's kingdom.
- Timothy had a proven and impeccable character that was witnessed by many.
- Timothy was an energetic encourager who went about strengthening the body of Christ.

The Challenges Timothy Faced:

- Timothy's father was Greek and his mother was Jewish. He came from a family with mixed beliefs, but God used him mightily.
- Timothy was young but God connected him with the right mentors like Paul.
- Timothy may have been challenged by fear since he was encouraged to be strong many times.
- Timothy was given much by God and was responsible for bringing order to different churches.

The Magnitude of Timothy's Task:

- How could this man from different backgrounds overcome the ridicule and be great for God?
- Timothy encountered people who probably looked down on his age. He did not let people despise his youth, he was just a good example before them.
- How does one get connected to great mentors? All things are possible with God.
- Being responsible for much can be overwhelming and taxing. Timothy had to learn how to trust God to overcome difficult challenges.

1. Heroic Quality One – Timothy had Rich Faith

As a believer in Christ you are to live and walk by faith not by sight. Timothy came from a rich heritage of faith where he was infused with faith from a faithful grandmother and mother. They taught Timothy the Word of God and trained him in the way he should go. Paul recognized that Timothy had a genuine faith in him (2 Tim 1:3-7). His rich faith made him a hero for God.

Timothy encouraged people to have pure motives: let love be your reason why you do good things; maintain a pure heart and keep a good conscience; live a clean life; remove dark secrets from your life; keep your faith real and sincere. Your faith should be like a child in believing God (1 Timothy 1:3-7).

Faith is a learning process that continues your whole life. You can increase your faith and continue to develop it by revisiting the basics of faith even though you are effective in living by faith. Timothy learned the Scriptures as a child that gave him knowledge of salvation. The word of God is the foundation for every good work. It inspires, teaches, reproves, corrects and instructs in righteousness (2 Timothy 3:14-17).

Paul referred to Timothy as a true son in the faith (1 Timothy 1:2). Paul sent Timothy to places to encourage and establish people in faith so that they are not shaken in afflictions (1 Thessalonians 3:2-3).

The Heroic Characteristic of Faith in the Scriptures

Paul encouraged Timothy to be a man of faith. Rich faith is sincere, genuine and comes from God's Word. God is rich in faith and faithful even when His children are not. God lavishly pours grace out where there is a reservoir of rich faith (1 Timothy 1:5, 12, 14; 2 Timothy 1:5; 2:13; 3:15).

A good conscience and a clean life keep faith strong. Greed and covetousness diminish and weaken faith. Good teaching on faith nourishes you in every area of life. By faith, you can do what is right; even if everyone else is doing what is wrong. Developing your faith is a worthy pursuit (1 Timothy 1:19; 6:10-11 4:6, 12; 2 Timothy 2:22; 3:10).

Faith is an important component and a powerful weapon to help you fight your spiritual battles and win. Your love and your lifestyle greatly affect faith and help you to establish right patterns of behavior. If you want to teach others about faith then be a good example and practice what you preach. In the last days, many will leave a lifestyle of faith. Do not be one of them! Faith is extremely precious and valuable so maintain it throughout your entire life. Perhaps you will be entered into the Great Hall of Faith like the one in Hebrews Ch. 11 (1 Timothy 6:12; 4:1; 2 Timothy 1:13; 2:2; 4:7).

Develop and strengthen your faith to do great exploits for God. Start living by faith now and be an everyday hero for God.

2. Heroic Quality Two – Timothy had a Great Work Ethic

Paul really loved Timothy and was very involved in his life. Paul first met him in Lystra. The believers there spoke well of Timothy and Paul wanted Timothy to travel with him. Timothy was a disciple who served the Lord. The apostle Paul saw something in Timothy and gave him the opportunity to assist him in ministry. **The work of Paul and Timothy did, strengthened the churches in faith and increased their numbers daily**. God connects you with the right people to accomplish great things in the earth (Acts 16:1-5).

Timothy also worked with Silas who was with Paul when God shook the prison in Philippi. It is awesome to see how God took this young disciple; put him with great mentors; so he could become a great minister too. When Paul was sent away from Berea, Timothy and Silas stayed there to minister to the churches there, until Paul wanted them to come to Athens. **Paul had confidence in these two protégé's** (Acts 17:14-15).

Timothy was involved in a network of ministers that traveled to many places preaching the word of God (Acts 19:21-22). Another person that Timothy worked with was Erastus. Erastus was the treasurer of a city, (Romans 16:23) and he ended up serving in Corinth (1 Timothy 4:20). Paul sent these two young men to Macedonia while he stayed in Asia for a while.

Paul referred to Timothy as a fellow worker (Romans 16:21). When Paul needed someone to teach the church at Corinth, He sent Timothy to them. He described Timothy as his *"dearly loved"* and *"faithful son in the Lord"*. Timothy was sent to remind the Corinthians about Paul's ways in Christ Jesus. Timothy represented Paul's heart and taught what Paul taught. He was a good worker for the Lord (1 Corinthians 4:16-17). Paul also told them that Timothy was doing the Lord's work just as he was doing (1 Corinthians 16:10).

Timothy was faithful to serve Paul and follow his instructions. He shared Paul's heart and mindset towards the people to which he ministered. Timothy was a good minister because he cared for people and was not covetous or greedy. Paul had such confidence in Timothy that he could send him anywhere and knew that his work produced good results (Philippians 2:19-24).

Timothy was a hero for God because he worked well and smart. His work produced good results.

The Heroic Characteristic of Work in the Scriptures

The Bible describes a good worker like this: As a good worker you are faithful to your boss and what you do for your employer; you are obedient to your boss; the work you do should come from a heart to please God; respect your boss whether he is good or evil. You do not have perform evil deeds, but respect the authority your boss has; do not compromise what you know is right; finally, be submissive (Proverbs 27:18; Ephesians 6:5; Colossians 3:22; 1 Timothy 6:1; Titus 2:9; 1 Peter 2:18).

A Hero works diligently because he usually works in an emergency situation. Adrenaline flows to act quickly to save lives. Timothy was a hero because he was a good worker. Do the Lord's work with a right attitude and you can be an everyday hero for God.

3. Heroic Quality Three – Timothy had Impeccable Character

It is God's desire that all His children develop good, godly and sound character. Only those with good moral character can really be trusted and relied upon by others. Heroes need to be people of strong character. Power corrupts and absolute power corrupts absolutely. Also, with great power comes great responsibility.

It is a powerful thing when a mentor can transfer his character and skill into another. Paul transferred his character and skill to Timothy. Paul traveled with Timothy, taught him like a father teaches his son, and sent him out on his own knowing that Timothy would represent him well. Only a person with impeccable character could represent another without seeking power or prestige for themselves. He was like-minded with his mentor Paul, who had proven Timothy's character and he knew he would take good care of the people (Philippians 2:19-24).

Paul was confident that Timothy's teaching would edify the people (1 Corinthians 4:16-17). It is awesome to think that when Paul sent Timothy to places, they were getting a *"little Paul"*, because Timothy represented and resembled him so well. Paul considered Timothy to be a fellow worker (1 Corinthians 16:10).

Timothy served the apostle Paul, traveled as a missionary, did the work of an evangelist and encouraged and strengthened the body of Christ wherever he went. If he had weak character, Paul would have confronted him about it. Paul was able to send him to different places because he knew Timothy. Timothy was his son in the faith and he was a well-trained disciple of the Lord and of Paul. Timothy's character made him a super hero for God.

The Heroic Characteristic of Character in the Scriptures

- Character reflects God's nature and it is profitable to be godly (1 Timothy 4:8)
- Character is who you are, wherever you are, and it flows out of your relationship with Christ.
- Character is wholeheartedly trusting in God and having a good conscience (1 Timothy 1:19)
- Character is abiding in God's standard not man's standard (1 Timothy 3:1-7)
- Character development is a worthy pursuit (1 Timothy 6:11-14)
- Character positively influences people, being an example to follow (1 Timothy 4:12-16)

- Character leads you to prosperity and success (Daniel, Mordecai, and Joseph)
- Character is developed by speaking God's Word, meditating in it, observing it and doing it (Joshua1:8)
- A lack of character leads to self-destruction (1 Samuel 2:27-36)
- Character is consistent and proven behavior over a period of time (Titus 2:7)

4. Heroic Quality Four – Timothy was a Godly Encourager

Timothy was a great encourager to people because his life was rooted and grounded in the Word of God. As an encourager: continue in what you have learned and been assured of; live for God; inspire others with your example.

Timothy learned God's Word at a young age. He probably memorized many Scriptures. He understood how profitable the Word of God was: to learn from; to teach; to reprove and correct wrong thinking and wrong acting; to equip a person to do God's work (2 Timothy 2:14-17).

Paul started many churches and considered himself to be a "wise master builder." **He knew how to establish a church, grow a church and keep a church strong**. After starting a church in one place, Paul would put a pastor there to lead that church, so he could go and start other churches in other places.

Timothy's first mission trip with Paul resulted in churches being strengthened in the faith and their numbers increasing daily. Godly encouragement develops strong faith. Godly mentorship multiplies the effects of godly encouragement. Timothy learned how to encourage others from his mentor, an expert encourager, Paul. God enabled Timothy to received Paul's ability to encourage others. The encouraging letters Paul wrote to churches then, are still encouraging churches today because they are in the Bible!

That is powerful.

An encourager continually reminds believers Who Christ is and what He has done, who they are in Him and what He has promised them. As an encourager, you build others up and cheer them on to become great! The message of the encourager is: powerful; truthful; uncompromising; genuine and real.

Paul could send Timothy to any church, knowing those believers would be built up in the ways of Jesus. An encourager always points people to Christ - who is the **Master Encourager**. Knowing Christ and His ways is the best way to encourage others. Finally, an encourager washes people with the Word of God. The best book of encouragement is the Bible (1 Corinthians 4:16).

Godly encouragement helps to establish believers in the faith of Jesus. Strong and established faith prevents you from being shaken when bad things happen. Established faith has been tested, tried and proven victorious. Thank God for the encouragers he sends across your path to establish and strengthen your faith to endure (1 Thessalonians 3:1-4).

The Heroic Characteristic of Encouragement in the Scriptures

- Moses encouraged the people to be fearless; stand still; see God's salvation (Exodus 14:13)
- God tells you to strengthen weak hands and make firm feeble knees by encouraging them (Isaiah 35:3)
- The Lord promises to hold your right hand; be fearless; He will help you (Isaiah 41:13)
- Jesus encouraged believers by telling them to be of good cheer; do not fear (Matthew 14:27)
- If you are troubled, Jesus will reveal Himself to you to calm your heart (Luke 24:36-42)
- You can overcome inner turmoil and depression by praising God and putting your hope in Him (Psalm 43:5).
- God comes along your side; to help you take heart; for it will be good (Acts 27:22)

Timothy was a hero because he encouraged people in the Lord, in the faith and in His word. You can encourage others also to be an everyday hero for God.

To help you understand the heroic qualities that Timothy possessed to make him an everyday hero, consider the following questions and answer them sincerely and make any adjustments that need to be made.

Questions to consider for your personal growth about being an everyday hero like Timothy

1. What stage of life were you in when you first had faith in Christ Jesus? Did you grow up in a godly home?

2. How has your faith developed over the years? How has your faith changed your life?

3. If people who know you commented on the quality of your work, what do you think they would say?

4. How well do you honor your boss and how well do you represent the company you work for?

5. How would people around you describe your character?

6. What are some ways and things you could do to strengthen your character?

7. When people encounter you in person, are they strengthened or weakened?

8. What are some ways you encourage your family, your friends, your co-workers or strangers?

9. Who mentors you? Who are you mentoring? What results are you experiencing?

10. What are some of the ways that Jesus has encouraged you?

The characters in this book were real people who really existed. They had God-given qualities, super powers, which made them godly heroes. Perhaps you share many good things in common with the characters in this book. I am confident that God has created you with your own super powers and He will help you to recognize and develop them so you can become an everyday hero for Him. That means you live for Him; love Him; serve Him and fight for Him every day.

It is possible for a man to be an everyday hero for God. Every day you can meet the challenges of life with overcoming power of God operating in you to cause you to do great things.

I want you to be an everyday hero for God. Take the pledge and commit to being an everyday hero for the Lord.

The Hero's Pledge

I commit to being an everyday hero for God by knowing God, His will, His way and following after Him with all my heart. I will use my God-given abilities as God leads me to help people and serve in His kingdom. I will be strong in character that promotes righteousness and justice believing and upholding what God says. I am an everyday hero for God. I live by faith and can do all things through Christ who strengthens me.

Bibliography

(Hitchcock's Bible Names Dictionary, PC Study Bible formatted electronic database Copyright © 2003 Biblesoft, Inc. All rights reserved.)

(from Nelson's Illustrated Bible Dictionary, Copyright (c)1986, Thomas Nelson Publishers)

(Nimitz-class aircraft carrier (2015, September 20. In Wikipedia), The Free Encyclopedia. Retrieved 23:38, October 1, 2015, from https://en.wikipedia.org/w/index.php?title=Nimitz-class_aircraft_carrier&oldid=682007287).

(from The New Unger's Bible Dictionary. Originally published by Moody Press of Chicago, Illinois. Copyright (c) 1988.).

(from Matthew Henry's Commentary on the Whole Bible: New Modern Edition, Electronic Database. Copyright (c) 1991 by Hendrickson Publishers, Inc.)

Jamieson-Fausset-Brown Bible Commentary

As an Agagite, Haman was a descendant of Agag, an Amalekite king whom God commanded Saul to destroy because of his wickedness. Samuel was the one who killed him (1 Samuel 15; Ex 17:16; Deuteronomy 25:19)

Cup-bearer (2015, January 28). In Wikipedia, The Free Encyclopedia. Retrieved 23:46, September 1, 2015, from https://en.wikipedia.org/w/index.php?title=Cup-bearer&oldid=644611436

ABOUT THE AUTHOR

Douglas Pyszka is passionate about helping people from all walks of life find their inheritance in the Word of God. He has traveled to Africa, South America, Europe and throughout North America helping people experience God's benefits. He is a 92' graduate of Rhema Bible Training College in Tulsa, OK and a 96' graduate of Lee University in Cleveland, TN. He currently serves as Senior Pastor of Victory Christian Fellowship (VCF), in Palmyra PA with his wife Fiona. They have been married for eighteen years and have two sons, Gabriel and Josiah. Douglas continues to share God's inheritance to people at VCF and abroad.

Made in the USA
Lexington, KY
07 October 2018